T5-AFL-757

Five Celebrated Early Surgeons

of
Southern Alberta
1874-1913

by
Dr. Robert Lampard

Publication Coordinator/Designer
Carlton R. Stewart

Occasional Paper No. 43
part of the Lethbridge Historical Society
publication program helping celebrate the
Centennial of Lethbridge
as a city in 2006

published by the
Lethbridge Historical Society
Chapter of the Historical Society of Alberta
P. O. Box 974 Lethbridge, Alberta, Canada T1J 4A2
2006
Produced with the facilities of the Lethbridge Historical Society
and the George and Jessie Watson Memorial Computer Centre.
Printed in Canada by Graphcom Printers - Lethbridge, Alberta

Front Cover
    Twelve o'clock - Dr. Richard Barrington Nevitt, MD   Glenbow Archives NA-2859-1
    Two o'clock - Dr. George Allan Kennedy, MB   Glenbow Archives NA-227-1
    Five o'clock - Dr. Leverett George deVeber, MD   Galt Archives GP19694786000
    Seven o'clock - Dr. George Henry Malcolmson, MD   University of Alberta Archives (Jamieson Collection) 81-104-77
    Ten o'clock - Dr. Frank Hamilton Mewburn, OBE, MD, FFACS, CM, LLD   Galt Archives GP19760229039

Rear Cover
    Top: Henri Julien, *The Doctor in his Tent,* 1875, Collection of Glenbow Museum, Calgary, Canada. Julien accompanied the NWMP on their trek as a
        illustrator for the Canadian Illustrated News. It is believed that the Doctor in the tent is R. Barrington Nevitt.
    Lower: Henri Julien, *Sick Parade* 1874, Collection of Glenbow Museum, Calgary, Canada. Dr. R. Barrington Nevitt is featured at the right, as he attends
        another member of the Force during sick parade.

This edition was prepared on Society computer equipment into page format and design. Galt Museum photographic
images were scanned on equipment partially sponsored by the Lethbridge Historical Society at the George and Jessie
Watson Computer Centre of the Museum.

Copyright © 2006 Lethbridge Historical Society City of Lethbridge

First printing
April 2006

Library of Archives of Canada Cataloguing in Publication

Lampard, Robert, 1940-
        Five celebrated early surgeons of Southern Alberta 1874-1913 / by Robert
Lampard ; publication coordinator/designer, Carlton R. Stewart.

(Occasional paper ; no. 43)
Includes bibliographical references and index.
ISBN 0-9780505-0-9

    1. Nevitt, Richard Barrington, 1850-1928. 2. Kennedy, George Allan, 1858-1913.
3. Mewburn, Frank Hamilton. 4. Malcolmson, George Henry. 5. DeVeber, Leverett
George, 1849-1927. 6. Surgeons--Alberta--Biography. I. Stewart, Carton R. (Carlton
Ross), 1937- II. Lethbridge Historical Society III. Title. IV. Series: Occasional paper
(Lethbridge Historical Society) ; no. 43.

RD27.34.L35 2006   617'.092'27123   C2006-901395-0

Dedication

Dr. Robert Lampard
President - Alberta Medical Foundation

This Occasional Paper is dedicated to the five frontier physicians who started medicine in Alberta, and to three colleagues of mine who came later.

The first colleague is Dr. Hugh A. Arnold MD, FACP, FRCP(C), whose commitment and contribution to the Alberta Medical Association was steadfast, unwavering and invariably given without question. His wise counsel and insight always stemmed from the clear vision he could articulate, when faced with any of the challenges he was asked to resolve by the AMA during his and after his 1963-64 year as President. One of his challenges was to take the concept of an autonomous institution devoted to preserving the history of medicine in Alberta and give it form, a form that became the Alberta Medical Foundation.

The second colleague is Alberta's first medical sociologist, the learned Brigham Young Card. Ph.D. Through his recollections and observations, he gave personality to the famous 1932 Cardston Medical Contracts. More importantly he helped put that story into its context, as part of the evolution of Medicare in Canada. The Cardston debate on January 3, 1932 and the Cardston medical insurance program that followed, placed the depression exacerbated limitation of access to medical care - back on the United Farmers of Alberta government's agenda in March of 1932. The first political/professional agreement on health insurance in Canada was reached by the end of 1932. It became the template for Medicare in Canada. In so doing Dr. Card highlighted the town of Cardston's social consciousness, and its ability to form an opinion and take decisive action on this very important Canadian healthcare issue. From it came the demonstration of the magic of medical insurance, a concept Alberta physicians successfully nationalized through the Canadian Medical Association.

The third colleague is the accomplished member of the Raymond, Alberta medical community and 2000/01 AMA President, Dr. Clayne Steed. In a magnanimous gesture, he disqualified himself from being considered as one of the 100 Alberta Physicians of the Century, by agreeing to chair the selection committee. In 2005 when Dr. Steed gave the keynote addresses to the two gala ceremonies in Calgary and Edmonton, he did it by telling the compelling story of how early southern Alberta medical care influenced his own family. Dr. Steed's story follows ... verbatim.

- - - - -

"In January 1905, eight months before Alberta became a province, my grandparents were married. Their first home was near the US-Canada border close by Outpost Lake in Alberta (now known a Police Lake). Built by my grandfather and his brother they moved into this log home in March 1905. With the imminent birth of a child in 1906 my grandmother went to the closest town, Cardston, some 25 miles away. Staying with friends, my grandmother had access to medical care for the birth of her first child. The same pattern was followed for a second child and the same was planned for a third child in 1910. However Fall work and the precipitous arrival of the third child meant he was born in the cabin. Complications followed, the proprieties of those of this generation left no record of the nature of the problems. My grandfather rode by horseback to a neighbour's home with the intention of changing horses and continuing on to Cardston. They, in the spirit of the times, sent him home, with the neighbour traveling the remaining miles to Cardston. Dr. Stackpool, a physician in Cardston at that time, then made the return trip by horse and sleigh to the log home some 25 miles distant from Cardston. My grandmother's history records that Dr. Stackpool saved her life and that of her son. This was a good thing as my mother was born in 1915.

While far from the first, Dr. Stackpool was but one of the early pioneer physicians in south Alberta. The demands of this new corner of Canada required the best and it attracted the best. There was an adventuring spirit, a pioneering spirit that came with these physicians. They were innovative, compassionate, dedicated and progressive. Interestingly they were diverse in their interests and accomplishments. Progressive in medicine but also part of the community, their contributions extended to other elements of community life in pioneer south Alberta.

History records the broad strokes of their lives. They went here, they did that. This hospital was built, this procedure was done. All of this is important and not to be forgotten. Be it in the practice of medicine or in the community, their impact and leadership contributed to the early fabric of Alberta.

Not to be missed however are the fine strokes, the detail of their lives. The fine strokes are the difference they made in the lives of individuals and families. Not subject to the same detail of recorded history but nevertheless of paramount significance is the impact they had on the lives of pioneer families. Often they were the difference between health and infirmity, life or death. The well-being of a mother in childbirth, the health and strength of a father following an accident, the preservation of the family circle when a child was sick; this was the readily accepted responsibility that rested upon the shoulders of these early physicians. Unfailingly they responded, leaving this generation to bear a perhaps unknown debt to those early physicians of south Alberta."

Dr. Clayne Steed - Past President, AMA
Selection Committee Chairman
100 Alberta Physicians of the Century

Table of Contents

Acknowledgements

The author and the Lethbridge Historical Society wish to recognize the organizations and individuals who have contributed financially to producing this publication. These donations are applied directly toward the costs of printing, allowing the public and schools to purchase the book at a much reduced cost.

Alberta Historical Resources Foundation

Provides annual grants to the Historical Society of Alberta for publishing. The Lethbridge Society will use their portion towards publishing at least four publications in 2006, celebrating the Centennial of Lethbridge.

Campbell Clinic of Lethbridge

Remembering Dr. deVeber who invited Dr. Peter Campbell to Lethbridge in 1906 to found the oldest continuing Clinic west of Winnipeg.

Bigelow Fowler Clinic of Lethbridge

In memory of our early pioneer surgeons and physicians who led the way.

Lethbridge Surgical Society

Recognizing the early pioneer surgeons who led the way.

Dr. Robert Lampard

To my father who grew up in Magrath, and to my Aunt Dorothy Lampard, one of the first Senators of the University of Lethbridge.

Anonymous

Donations have been received from persons who wish to remain unknown.

Primary acknowledgement for identifying the pioneering role of the physicians in Southern Alberta must go to Dr. Heber Jamieson. His careful research and many one of a kind photographs, punctuate the two articles he wrote on Early Doctors in Southern Alberta (CMAJ 38: 391-397, 1938) and on Southern Alberta Medicine in the 1880s (CMAJ 54: 391-396, 1946) and this one.

One half a century later, Dr. Gerald McDougall had the foresight to study the Medical Clinics and Physicians in Southern Alberta. Four of the nine clinics were in Lethbridge. More importantly he interviewed senior members of all nine medical clinics, before publishing his book in 1991. The book included a chapter (pages 89-95) on Early Medicine in Lethbridge.

The third acknowledgement must go to the Lethbridge Historical Society for starting the occasional paper series and for enticing avocational historians like Dr. Alex Johnston to undertake the original research on medicine in Lethbridge (Occasional Paper #24) in 1991.

The last acknowledgement must go to the persistent, knowledgeable, experienced editor of the occasional paper series, Carlton (Carly) Stewart, who gave this project the time and energy it required to be completed.

My thanks particularly to those individuals, organizations and clinics that defrayed the costs of sharing the stories of five significant Southern Alberta medical pioneers.

Dr. Robert Lampard

Our photographs were obtained from: Sir Alexander Galt Museum and Archives (Galt Archives) of Lethbridge where Greg Ellis was of considerable help during a particular hectic time at the Galt. And from the Jamieson Collection of the University of Alberta Archives in Edmonton, the Glenbow Museum, in Calgary and from Dr. Lampard's private collection or sources.

The Lethbridge Historical Society wish to thank the following for their continued help and support: Book Committee members Jean Johnstone - President, Barry Snowden - Past President, Councillors - Audrey Swedish & Bill Lingard and in particular Treasurer David Dowey who's close scrutiny and candid insight are most welcomed.

Computer specialist, John Fisher for his task which is easy to him but mind boggling to me and to Marla Stewart for her assistance in searching the Galt and Glenbow photo web sites.

Graphcom Printers are a resource we lean on for all of our publications; they continue to provide us with excellent service, and a quality timely product.

Dr. A.R.F. (Eric) Williams, society member and a resource person that we asked to seek financial support from his colleagues within the Medical Community of Lethbridge, allowing you the reader to buy the publication at reduced costs. Dr. Williams also reviewed the manuscript on two of more occasions.

Carly Stewart - Book Committee Chair
Lethbridge Historical Society

Introduction

Dr. Robert Lampard, MD

Medicine in southern Alberta holds a unique place in the annals of medical history of this province. It is where the practice of medicine began. Medical imprints are visible in southern Alberta from 1859 onward, as the province evolved from a migratory aboriginal territory through the fur trade, NWMP, CPR construction, and permanent settlement eras, to the birth of Alberta in 1905. Four of the five surgeons were brought to Alberta by the North West Mounted Police.

The first medical practitioner that actually came to the North West was an explorer and geographer. Dr. James Hector visited the Blackfoot country in the summer of 1859. He traversed the arid Palliser triangle and concluded it was smaller than expected. En passant he treated the ill Indians presented to him. His remedies were limited. They included tea for diarrhea and strychnine to kill the menacing wolves at night.

The featured five were chosen because of the indelible marks they left on medicine and their Southern Alberta communities. Three (Kennedy, Mewburn, deVeber) formed a team that extended medical care to include major surgery. All five became specialists (Nevitt - Obstetrics and Gynecology, Kennedy - Medical Management, deVeber - Public Health, Mewburn - Surgery, Malcolmson - Radiology) and impacted medicine across Canada. They were outstanding examples of medical men who rose to the challenge of practicing medicine on the last frontier.

The first of the adventurous five physicians, came as part of the famous NWMP March. Dr. R. Barrington Nevitt arrived and helped construct Fort Macleod in October 1874. He was on a four year contract with the NWMP, to attend the sick parades, treat the walking wounded, address the injuries, the fractures, gun-shot accidents, and deal with the frozen limbs, pneumonias and infections. His practice included the NWMP men, their wives and families, the settlers and aboriginals. He extended the radius of his practice by being a competent horseman. No call was ever refused, in any season.

The greatest health challenges faced by Dr. Nevitt and his successors were the waves of epidemics that swept the plains. They ranged from influenza to diphtheria, smallpox, whooping-cough, and measles. With them came the imported diseases including syphilis, gonorrhea and later, tuberculosis.

In 1878 Dr. Nevitt was succeeded by Dr. George A. Kennedy, the first physician to come and stay in southern Alberta. Together with his son Alan, they provided three quarters of a century of continuous medical care to Fort Macleod. Dr. Kennedy arrived as a twenty year old silver medallist from the University of Toronto, too young to legally write a prescription. In 1884 he brought J.D. Higinbotham, the first pharmacist, to Alberta. Higinbotham would, in turn bring another assistant, the well-known Dr. Walter S. Galbraith.

The 1885 Northwest (Riel) Rebellion left its own medical imprint on southern Alberta. In the marshalling exercise, Dr. deVeber joined the Rocky Mountain Rangers. They policed the border and telegraph line to Medicine Hat without incident. Dr. Kennedy handled the Fort Macleod medical problems including joining a quickly raised militia unit to scour the surrounding territory for rumored armed Indian bands.

The weather of southern Alberta left its mark too. Dr. Frank Mewburn visited Lethbridge in December 1885, on the promise of an NWMP contract and a three bed hospital. He was impressed by the Chinook that greeted him. His arrival in January 1886 created a critical mass of physicians, namely three: a surgeon, an assistant surgeon and an anesthetist, Mewburn, Kennedy and deVeber. That was the number needed to perform elective and urgent surgery. In the absence of any trained nurses, Dr. Mewburn enlisted the help of families, friends or the nearest pair of hands to operate. Aftercare often required assistance from the physicians' wives. The well-read, audacious Mewburn and Kennedy undertook surgical operations not attempted in other Alberta settlements for another decade.

The early physicians always put patient care first and bills, if paid at all, second. Early private practices were supplemented by contracts with the NWMP, Galt mines, Department of Indian Affairs, and the CP Crowsnest and Great Falls railways. Population growth permitted Dr. L.G. deVeber to start the first private practice without a contract in Fort Macleod in 1885. deVeber was already well known because of his famous house call. While posted at Fort Macleod in the spring of 1883, he answered a son's call to visit his sick mother, 140 miles (200 kilometres) away in Morley, west of Calgary. His only prescription was the remaining brandy he had left in his flask, which the patient refused to the pleasure of Dr. deVeber.

The adventurous and multi-talented early physicians left their legacy in other ways. Dr. Nevitt was a self-taught watercolour artist, who painted the Indian treaty signings, Chiefs and notable gatherings. He was a diarist but unfortunately his annual reports and most of his diaries were lost. Only six month of letters to his future wife survive. They confirm he was a keen observer of people, the elements, the events and the health conditions of the time. Dr. Kennedy followed by researching the influence of the climate of southern Alberta on medical diseases. He gave the first NWT medical paper on the subject at the Canadian Medical Association annual meeting in Banff in 1889.

Dr. Kennedy was the chief medical organizer in the NWT, becoming the president of the NWT Medical Association in 1889, the first hospital inspector in 1897 and the president of the NWT Medical Executive Council from 1902 to 1906. During his presidency an agreement was reached with the NWT Legislative Council to build the first laboratory in the NWT (c1904). Dr. Kennedy petitioned the Minister of the Interior, Clifford Sifton to bring the second full-time physician to provide medical care for the Blood Indians in 1901, Dr. O.C. Edwards. He was successful. Kennedy was instrumental in resolving the problem of registering physicians with different backgrounds and MD qualifications. Described as the "western Roddick" he led the Canadian Medical Association to revisit the concept of a Medical Council of Canada (MCC). It was established in 1912 and still exists. Drs. Kennedy and Thomas Roddick were two of the three council members named to the first Board by the federal cabinet.

Dr. Kennedy orchestrated the renovation of the NWMP hospital at Fort Macleod in 1883. It had space to perform surgery. One of his first and most prominent cases was the local lawyer Mr. C.C. McCaul. McCaul accidentally shot himself through the chest a month after his marriage in 1886. McCaul taxed the abilities of Kennedy and Mewburn and their wives, to treat his contaminated chest injury and recurring chest infections, that required drainage, rib excisions and months of nursing care. In 1890 Kennedy and Mewburn operated on an NWMP carpenter, who had an un-united fracture of his leg. They used sterilized dog bone chips, which were unfortunately rejected and required another operation that shortened the leg but lasted another fifty years.

Dr. Mewburn was a self-taught surgeon. He was well-read and could research the procedure the night before and operate the next day. His superb collection of medical journals and texts became one of the collections that started the University of Alberta medical library. His string of surgical firsts were Alberta firsts. They ranged from abdominal drainages, to the first appendectomy, thyroidectomy, followed by hernias, ectopic pregnancies and caesarean sections, all before 1904. So pleased was Dr. Mewburn with his surgical results, that he polarized his practice solely to surgery in 1913, another Alberta first. That was the year he moved of the Calgary General Hospital.

Dr. Mewburn contributed to the life of Lethbridge as the Mayor for three years. He brought Dr. George Malcolmson to work for him for a year in 1898 before Malcolmson moved westward on a Crowsnest Pass CPR medical contract. Dr. Malcolmson built his own hospital as an annex to his home in Frank. It narrowly missed the swath of the Turtle Mountain slide in 1903. The dozen casualties that survived or were extracted from the debris were stabilized and treated there.

Love and respect for these frontier physicians was shown by their communities through the creation of the first foundations for healthcare, hospitals. In southern Alberta the appreciative citizens built the first public hospital with an OR in Alberta in Medicine Hat in 1889, and the second in Lethbridge in 1890-91. They were followed by the Calgary General Cottage Hospital in 1890, the Holy Cross Hospital in 1891 and the Edmonton General Hospital in 1896.

The southern Alberta medical practices for the five surgeons ranged from four years by Nevitt to thirty-five years by Kennedy. All were before WWI. The four who stayed, matured as their medical practices grew. They became leaders in their communities and gave freely of their time and competence. They sat on boards of trade, school boards and hospital boards. In sporting circles they initiated and participated in polo, golf and curling.

Their contributions continued after they left their practices in southern Alberta. Nevitt became the head of surgery at the Women's College Hospital in Toronto and delivered a baby a day for the rest of his life. deVeber became the first physician in the Alberta cabinet, before being appointed the first physician Senator from Alberta in 1906. Malcolmson became the first radiologist in Alberta and the first director of a free cancer clinic program in Canada. Mewburn self enlisted and became the head of surgery at one of Canada's WWI general hospitals in Europe. Underneath him were numerous future heads of surgery. Alongside him was his friend Sir William Osler. Mewburn returned to Alberta and became University of Alberta's first professor of surgery.

As we look back over the first century of medicine in Alberta, the strength of the pillars on which it is founded are remarkable. Here are five of them.

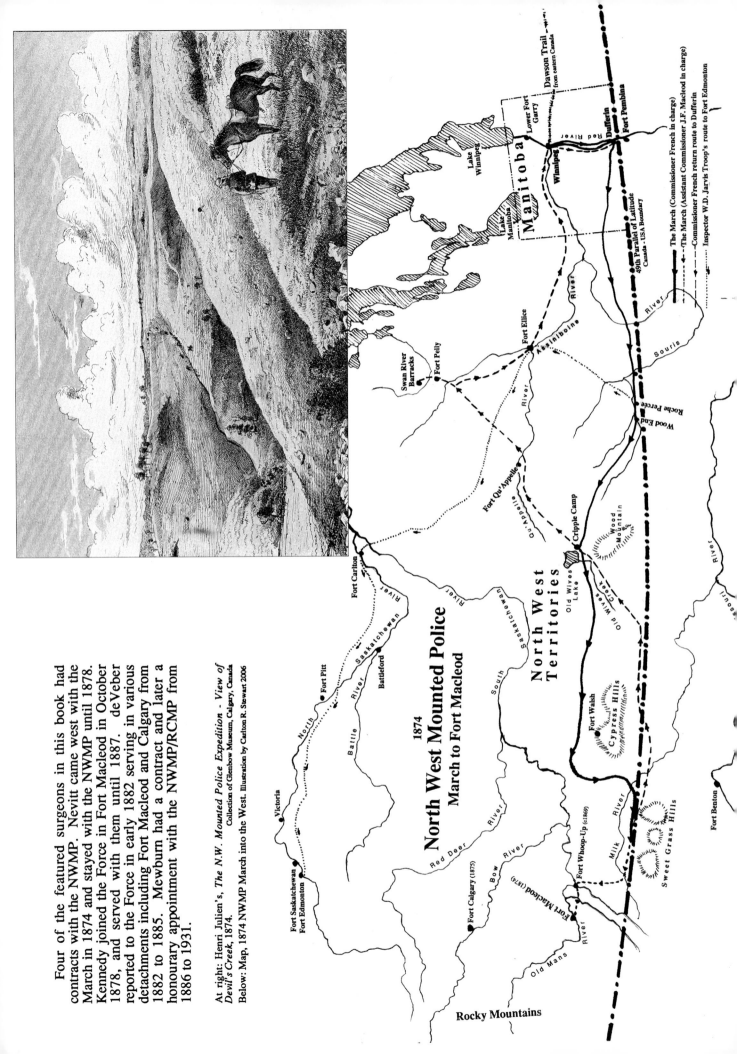

Four of the featured surgeons in this book had contracts with the NWMP. Nevitt came west with the March in 1874 and stayed with the NWMP until 1878. Kennedy joined the Force in Fort Macleod in October 1878, and served with them until 1887. deVeber reported to the Force in early 1882 serving in various detachments including Fort Macleod and Calgary from 1882 to 1885. Mewburn had a contract and later a honourary appointment with the NWMP/RCMP from 1886 to 1931.

At right: Henri Julien's, *The N.W. Mounted Police Expedition - View of Devil's Creek, 1874.*
Collection of Glenbow Museum, Calgary, Canada

Below: Map, 1874 NWMP March into the West. Illustration by Carlton R. Stewart 2006

Glenbow Archives NA-2859-1

Dr. Richard Barrington Nevitt, MD
1850 - 1928
The NWT Years 1874-1878
(He)...spurned the tedium of the trodden ways.[1]

Introduction

The 1874 NWMP March was a major milestone in Canadian prairie history. Over three hundred new recruits marched 1,000 miles in four months from Dufferin, Manitoba to Fort Macleod and established law and order in the North West Territories. At the Sweet Grass Hills, west of the Cypress Hills, the Troop divided. The smaller Division returning under Commissioner G.A. French, to winter at Swan River, Manitoba. The larger Division carried on under Assistant Commissioner J.F. Macleod to an empty Fort Whoop-Up near Lethbridge before continuing to the site for Fort Macleod.

Not well known is that the March included two American-born, Canadian-trained physicians, Surgeon Dr. John Kittson and his 24 year-old Assistant Surgeon Dr. Richard Barrington Nevitt. Both had signed four year contracts before accompanying the police. The two surgeons were the vanguard of full-time surgeons. After the CPR crossed the prairies in 1882/83, the NWMP began joint-contracting with the Department of Indian Affairs and with local physicians as they arrived in the NWT, on a part-time basis.[2] At smaller detachments, they hired junior "physicians" as Hospital Sergeants.[3]

The benefit of having two physicians on the March was evident from the start. The first week out of Dufferin the March was almost halted. There was an outbreak of diarrhea and dysentery. Several men were returned to Dufferin. Strict hygiene measures aborted the outbreak and saved the March. The disease, called Red River, Mountain, unremitting, or typhomalaria fever was a variable presentation of typhoid fever. It would become the commonest cause of NWMP deaths. The total would reach twenty-three of the ninety-six NWMP deaths between 1886-1900. This did not include the

deaths of the two men on the March, many civilian deaths, or any NWMP deaths from 1874-1885, as records for those years are not available.

As soon as Assistant Commissioner James F. Macleod and his Division arrived at their destination, men of the NWMP built a two hundred foot perimeter Fort in October/November 1874 and named it Fort Macleod. It contained a freestanding hospital, which might better be described as a single room large enough for ten or twelve cots. It was the second hospital on the western prairies, built two years after the first Cottage Hospital of twenty beds, opened in Winnipeg in 1872.

Surgeon Nevitt didn't wait for patients to arrive. Whether it was in sunshine or in a storm, he responded to all emergencies over the next three and one-half years. He became an expert horseman. He needed to be. Many times he would have been lost at night or in whiteouts. Like the rest of the Force, he soon found that the red uniform was too hot in the summer and far too cold in the winter.

While the primary duties of the NWMP surgeons was to meet the needs of the NWMP personnel, they also provided medical services to more than forty to fifty thousand settlers, families, Metis and Indians, within reach of the Forts. Their medical expertise was challenged by the waves of epidemics and infections that swept the prairies: small-pox, influenza, measles, and on a smaller scale typhoid fever, dysentery, gonorrhea, diphtheria and tuberculosis.

Between calls and trips with Lt. Colonel Macleod to as far away as Morley, near Banff, Dr. Nevitt had time on his hands. He put it to good use. Besides his regular sick parades, he wrote monthly hospital reports, prepared annual reports of his sick parades and listed the diagnoses of the men requiring hospitalization. He wrote to his fiancée he had left behind in Toronto. His "Dear Lizzy" letters averaged one every two days, over his first six months at Fort Macleod. They were the only letters that have survived from Nevitt's four years on the prairies. They portray Dr. Nevitt as a keen observer and a systematic documentor of weather, geography and the passing parade. In one letter Nevitt noted the reputation of the American west for having a healthy dry climate, was just as applicable to the southern Canadian prairies.

Nevitt must have brought pigments, dyes and brushes with him, for he began to paint scenes and gatherings when they occurred. In his four years at Fort Macleod, he created over 107 sketches and paintings. Many are one of a kind records of: Treaty-signings, portraits of Chiefs, etc.

On the 100th Anniversary of the NWMP Trek in 1974, the Glenbow Foundation of Calgary assembled the first exhibit of Nevitt watercolors. To complement the exhibit, Lizzy's six months of letters were published in "A Winter at Fort Macleod",[4] as was Dr. John Kittson's 1874 March report in "A Chronicle of the Canadian West".[5]

The NWMP formation and trek west, was originally to be short lived. But the NWMP were so effective in establishing law and order, and responding to the second Riel (NW) Rebellion of 1885, that the NWMP were continued as the RNWMP 1904-1920 and RCMP (after 1920). The "Force" received "Royal" designation in 1904.

From Youth to Bachelor of Medicine (MB)

Richard Barrington "Barrie" Nevitt was born in Savannah, Georgia, USA on November 22, 1850. Initially schooled in Savannah, he arrived in Montreal with his sister, as a fourteen year old in 1864. Like many other Southern USA children, the Nevitt children were sent to Canada during the last year of the Civil War, as the devastation and destruction by the Northern Armies reached Georgia.[6]

In 1865 Nevitt enrolled in Bishop's College School in Lennoxville, Quebec. By 1867 he was a 'head boy' and was excelling in athletics. In 1868 he graduated and transferred to Toronto's Trinity College, where he met another student, William Osler, whose example and advice may have influenced his own career choice.[7] Nevitt graduated from University of Toronto (UofT) with a Bachelor of Arts in 1871, and immediately entered Trinity Medical College. He received his Bachelor of Medicine (MB) in 1874. Dr. Nevitt's medical interest lay in obstetrics. He thought of specializing in it under Oliver Wendell Holmes in Boston and the Paul Semmelweis group in Vienna. His friends discouraged him from traveling to war-torn Europe. They encouraged him instead to obtain more medical experience. This circle of friends probably included William Osler.[8] Besides, Nevitt had steadily incurred a significant debt.

During his UofT years Nevitt joined the Trinity University Corps, a military unit of the Queen's Own Rifles "H" Company. He also gained "in hospital" experience at the Toronto General Hospital, by residing there and working as a dresser, pharmacy assistant and house surgeon.

May 1873, Forming The NWMP

In May 1873 the North West Mounted Police (NWMP) was formed. This Force was modeled like many peacekeeping forces of the time, based on the Royal Irish Constabulary. The Act provided for a mounted police force, which was to enter and traverse the Hudson's Bay Company (HBC) Territory (now Saskatchewan and Alberta), acquired by the Dominion of Canada from the HBC in 1870. The Act came into effect on August 30, 1873.[9] The NWMP were to establish law and order, control the whiskey trade with the Natives, then eventually disband. The original concept was to raise the Divisions in Manitoba, but there was insufficient response. More officers and men had to be recruited in Ontario.

The first one hundred and fifty recruits were sent to Manitoba in October 1873, via the already frozen Dawson Route or all-Canadian route across Lake of the Woods. NWMP Commissioner G.A. French led that March. On his arrival he went immediately to the Stone Fort (Fort Garry) in Winnipeg. There he discovered the Canada/US boundary survey teams were only 420 miles west of Dufferin (now Emerson) Manitoba, situated on the Red River as it crossed the U.S./Manitoba border. Beyond that point the only map was the Great Map from the Palliser Expedition, published in 1864.[10]

April 1874, The Beginning of the NWMP March

In April 1874 an additional sixteen officers and two hundred men were recruited in Ontario. The selection criteria was based on previous service in the Royal Irish Constabulary or training at the gunnery schools in Kingston and Quebec. One physician, Dr. John Kittson, had already been contracted to help select recruits. Kittson was the son of Commodore Kittson, who owned and ran the fleet of steamboats up and down the Red River supplying Winnipeg from Minnesota. It was likely the recruitment of the second contingent, that led to the signing of Dr. Nevitt as the second NWMP surgeon.

After graduation Nevitt was offered an opportunity to treat smallpox, infectious disease problems and patients in the lumbering area north of Orillia, Ontario. This position didn't require passing the Ontario registration exam. Nor did the NWMP position. The latter was his preference. Nevitt applied and was likely accepted by Dr. John Kittson. Nevitt, like Kittson was American born and Canadian (McGill) trained.

For Dr. Nevitt it was an opportunity for adventure, experience and to save money.[11] Nevitt contracted with the Force on July 6, 1874 at a remuneration of a thousand dollars per year. He left Toronto before his contract started and before the second contingent left Toronto. En route he stopped in St. Paul where he met Commodore Kittson.[12] Nevitt was advised to stay in Grand Forks, Minnesota because the Red River was still frozen. Dr. Nevitt remained there for ten days where he did a locumtenens.[13] Local rail construction workers rioted on Saturday night. A bullet intended for the superintendent, hit the local nurse in the thigh. Nevitt removed the bullet under local anesthesia, settling the crowd in the process.

The second contingent of NWMP recruits left Toronto on June 6, 1874. The two special trains carried 217 men and 244 horses. They traveled via Sarnia, Detroit, Chicago and St. Paul, before arriving at Fargo, North Dakota on June 12. Dr. Nevitt joined them in either Grand Forks or Fargo. Dr. John Kittson, who was with the second contingent treated one man for Erysipelas (a skin infection) and one recruit, who seizured. The latter was later discharged.[14] The troop headed north from Fargo on June 15. On the way several men developed diarrhea. It resolved with treatment. Arriving in Dufferin on June 19, they encountered a terrific thunderstorm on June 20. Two hundred and fifty-four horses broke their corrals and stampeded full tilt downwind for up to fifty miles. All the horses were later recovered, except one. One recruit suffered a serious skull laceration, which required extensive suturing.[15]

July 1874, NWMP March

During the first week of July 1874 the NWMP revolvers arrived from England.[16] This meant the Force could depart, which they did after a two day delay on the afternoon of July 8, 1874.[17] Drs. Nevitt and Kittson departed from Dufferin with the 318 man Force.[18] Two days later Nevitt headed back to Dufferin for a short time, to help treat a serious case of typhoid that had relapsed. The sick recruit had been left in the care of American physicians stationed across the US border in Pembina. This case heralded a bigger problem, a typhoid epidemic which spread throughout Manitoba. Later that winter in November 1874, after Dr. John Kittson had returned from Fort Macleod to Fort Ellice in Manitoba, he too developed typhoid fever. Kittson would be months recovering from it. Worse, he would acquire it again, when treating Inspector Sam Steele at Fort Walsh, NWT in the fall of 1879.

Nevitt was back on the NWMP March by July 11, only to face several more cases of diarrhea. Six were successfully treated but three has to be sent back to Dufferin. Dr. Nevitt accompanied them. One would die, as did the first case of typhoid. Nevitt was back for the third time and last time on the March by July 16.

The NWMP reached their geographic marker, Roche Percée, 270 miles west of Dufferin by July 26. By then their drug cupboard was being challenged.[19] Dr. Kittson had brought oil of Juniper to ward off mosquitoes. It worked to some extent. Liquid ammonium diluted ten times gave immediate relief. The "magnetic ointment" for sore skin was already used up.

Below: Henri Julien's sketch of the NWMP March as it approached the Sweet Grass Hills.   Galt Archives GP19871169000

At Roche Percée, Inspector Jarvis took a separate Detachment (Troop A) and headed north to Edmonton. He took with him four medical cases who were to return to Winnipeg: one phthisis, one prostatic abscess, a sprained ankle and a diarrhea patient. After forwarding the patients to Winnipeg, the Jarvis Troop continued the trek via Fort Ellice to Edmonton, arriving November 1, 1874.

On July 31, the remaining five divisions left Roche Percée. On August 2 diarrhea and dysentery again broke out amongst twenty-two NWMP personnel.[20] Two also developed pneumonia and were sent by wagon "ambulance" to Bismark, North Dakota for treatment. The rest of the cases cleared slowly.[21]

On August 12, Nevitt made a "house call" twelve miles distant to deliver a baby for a fifteen-year old Indian mother. She was at Wood Mountain, where Sitting Bull and 2,900 Sioux would later arrive in 1877, following the Custer massacre in 1876. The mother had a footling presentation which he diagnosed, and then he delivered a full-term daughter without difficulty.[22]

By August 19, 1874 the Force was at Crippled Camp, so called because seven cases were left to convalesce: an orchitis, a varicocele, three typhoid fevers, one diarrhea and a hand infection. Dr. Nevitt stayed with them for a short time. They were to be picked up by the returning Force under Commissioner French. By August 25 the March reached the Cypress Hills. This was the second marker point, 324 miles west of Rock Percée or six hundred miles west of Dufferin.

At the Cypress Hills, Dr. Nevitt discovered his medicine chest had several broken bottles of Chloroform and Carbolic Acid. It had to be repacked.[23] The next day Nevitt and Assistant Commissioner James Macleod took a side trip to meet with HBC officials and Indians. Dr. Nevitt also attended to several sick Indian patients.

On September 7 Nevitt and Commissioner Macleod scoured the Cypress Hills for a site for Fort Walsh. Nevitt choose the most sanitary location he could find and made plans for the construction of a hospital. Rejoining the troop on September 18, Nevitt found Dr. Kittson treating many members of the Force who had developed the flu, bronchitis, and various aches and pains. Kittson faced another problem, lice, which he successfully treated with the remaining Oil of Juniper.[24]

September 1874
The NWMP Splits at the Sweet Grass Hills

On September 22 the March was nine hundred miles "out" from Dufferin near the Sweet Grass Hills. Commissioner French, James Macleod, Drs. Kittson and Nevitt and a detachment, left the main Troop and headed for Fort Benton, Montana USA to secure money, supplies, letters and instructions. They took a recruit who was to be discharged. Upon their return to the main Force, Commissioner French with Chief Surgeon Kittson separated from the main Force and headed back east to the designated NWMP headquarters at Swan River, Manitoba, via Dufferin, arriving in Swan River, Manitoba on November 7, 1874 at minus 30ºF. By then Kittson and the NWMP men had traveled almost two thousand miles in four months. Kittson noted "there have been loss of oxen and horses, a few desertions and two deaths. All men had put on weight except one and that member was the better for it".[25]

From the Sweet Grass Hills, the Troop under Assistant Commissioner Lt. Colonel Macleod headed for Fort Whoop-Up (near Lethbridge) on the Old Man River. The Macleod Troop picked up famous Metis guide Jerry Potts on its way. On October 7, they rescued five whiskey traders from the Indians. On October 10, they found Fort Whoop-Up empty. Commissioner Macleod offered to buy the Fort but Whiskey Trader Dave Akers refused. The Troop went on. Three days later, Jerry Potts announced their arrival at the Old Man River, again. Macleod selected an island in the river as the site for the Fort. It became Fort Macleod, when the men voted to name it after their Assistant Commissioner. The NWMP Trek had covered almost one thousand miles in three months. The trek ended on October 13, 1874.

October 1874 - Arrival at Fort Macleod

The men immediately began to erect a wood enclosure for the two hundred foot square Fort. The log perimeter wall also served as the walls for many of the buildings. It was none too soon. The temperature dropped so low in November that the sick parade on one day reached forty-five (mostly colds). Eight men had to be transferred to other nearby Forts Kipp and Standoff. In December, with the help of a Chinook, the Fort was completed including a detached ten to twelve bed "hospital".[26] The photograph of the "Fort Calgary" hospital taken circa 1877 is representative of the hospital in Fort Macleod.[27] It consisted of one room with cots and a pot belly stove.

"Dear Lizzy" Letters,
October 11, 1874 to June 14, 1875[28]

In January 1875 Dr. Nevitt was bunked with a Trooper Allen. His father was Dr. W.C. Allen, the long time Mayor of Cornwall, Ontario and Customs Collector at Fort Macleod. Nine years later Nevitt's successor Dr. George A. Kennedy would meet and marry Allen's sister, Alice Maude Allen, after she came west to visit Trooper Allen.

During a storm in January 1875, Indians came to the Fort with news that two men had died. Nevitt went back with one of the Indians. They couldn't see a yard ahead. Luckily they managed to find one of the two bodies. Standard sick parades that winter averaged three men with two in the hospital. Frequent side trips by Dr. Nevitt were required to the nearby Forts of Standoff and Kipp, twenty miles each way.

In February Nevitt visited and befriended Chief Crowfoot. Nevitt decided to learn the Blackfoot language. Crowfoot paid Nevitt a return visit, having quite enjoyed the Seidlitz powder he gave him, because it fizzed and was therefore "very strong". When followed by a drink of ginger tea, it made Crowfoot tipsy. One Metis commented, "I'm glad I came here. They were all good to me and the little doctor is a smart doctor". Nevitt enjoyed the comments. On February 22,

1875 Dr. Nevitt finished his first written hospital report. It wasn't long before he was making yet another "tedious report", as he called them, for Dr. Kittson back in Swan River, Manitoba. And that month he also revisited Chief Crowfoot, who was quite ill.

In March 1875 Nevitt was delighted to get a bag of letters, forty-eight at once. In the same mail delivery he received his commission as a surgeon. He noted in one of his reports that the Morley trader David McDougall had begun to ship his trade goods to Fort Benton, instead of across the prairies to Winnipeg and Dufferin, because it was now a safer route.

In April 1875 Commissioner Macleod, with Major Walsh and Captain Cecil Denny, returned from Fort Benton and brought a small microscope. Dr. Nevitt said the power wasn't very high, but it would be useful in "botanizing". For pathological or physiological research, it would be "worse than useful". In the same mail he enjoyed receiving issues of the Canadian Monthly and a report from Dr. Joseph Workman the well-known Ontario psychiatrist. His medical supply ordered the previous October, also arrived. Nevitt noted they took so long to come, that he should be ordering his Fall's supply in the next letter out. He also had to complete another report on the medical department's activities for Dr. Kittson.

Dr. Nevitt must have participated in some private practice, as he noted he had "made over fifty dollars from outsiders". On June 13, 1875 he recorded he had three or four patients, some half-breeds.

Below: A page from Dr. Nevitt's diary of December 1877.

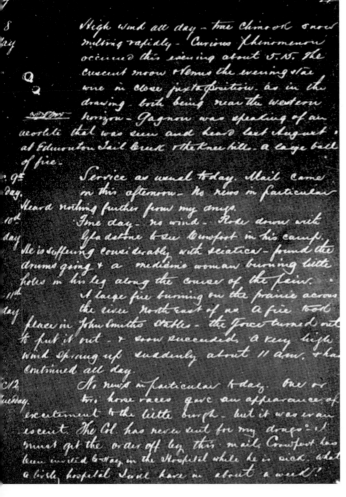

1874-1878   At Fort Macleod

In the winter of 1874/75 Nevitt made side trips west up the Old Man River to Lundbreck Falls, which he sketched. He also visited east to Fort Walsh to treat the casualties and injuries that had occurred there.

Later in 1875 Dr. Kittson, returned from Manitoba and toured Forts Walsh and Macleod. In late 1875 Inspector Brisbois was sent north from Fort Macleod to the Bow River to build a Fort. Unrest amongst the men developed at Fort Brisbois. Dr. Nevitt, Commissioner Macleod and Inspector A.G. Irvine traveled north in the spring of 1876 to investigate. Macleod changed the name from Fort Brisbois to Fort Calgary, and made other operational decisions that settled the Troops. On the same trip, Nevitt, Macleod and Irvine made a side venture west up the Bow River to the Rocky Mountains and Morleyville.

In 1875, Nevitt's brother Harry joined him and worked as a local trader in the area. Unfortunately Harry died three years later.

In March 1877, Dr. Nevitt made a trip to Calgary to examine two or three sick men. He noted the hospital "looks well". "Doc" John Lauder the Hospital-Sergeant presented a list of requirements. A box of drugs was sent to Lauder on February 26, 1878, completing his list.[29] Nevitt also packed a box of drugs for Hospital Sergeant G.F. Herchmer at Fort Saskatchewan, further north.

Chief Crowfoot took advantage of the Macleod Hospital, when he asked to be treated there in December 1877 for sciatica. A short time later Nevitt operated on a woman in Jerry Potts' house and removed a large piece of dead bone from the head of her upper arm.[30]

In September 1877 Dr. Nevitt was part of the NWMP contingent that attended the signing of Treaty #7 with Natives, at Blackfoot Crossing near Gleichen, Alberta. Nevitt made three sketches during the occasion.

In 1878 Nevitt was ordered to Fort Walsh. He met Inspector Irving and Chief Sitting Bull, who had come to Canada after the Custer massacre in 1877. Nevitt treated Dr. Kittson on February 12, 1878 (location unknown) and noted that "some more bone fragments came away this morning. Face is improving and strength getting better".

Most of Dr. Nevitt's journals have been lost. Only the journal diary from November 23, 1877 until the fall of 1878 has been discovered. There are no 1874-1878 NWMP reports by either Drs. Kittson or Nevitt. Apparently reports were written but were probably lost in an 1879 fire. Only the December 19, 1875 report, which was a two year medical report by Dr. John Kittson, has survived. It was written after his recovery from typhoid.[31]

The 1879 Report of Dr. John Kittson

Except for Dr. John Kittson's two year December 19, 1875 medical report, the earliest surviving NWMP reports after the 1874 March are those, by Surgeon Kittson at Fort Walsh, January 30, 1880 covering the year 1879[32] and Surgeon Kennedy at Fort Macleod,

November 30, 1879 covering his first year.[33] These reports remain representative examples of the medical care and treatment Dr. Nevitt would have provided at the time.[34]

Dr. Kittson described 1879 as a satisfactory year. The commonest medical parade cases were for climate related conditions: Catarrh, Influenza, and Rheumatism especially at the beginning of the year.[35] In the spring a mild form of Mountain Fever occurred throughout the Cypress Hills in both "remitting and intermittent" forms. The worst cases Kittson felt were similar to Typhoid with a prolonged and painful death in those it affected. No NWMP men died that year. Kittson noted that the first typhoid case appeared during the 1874 March. The first NWMP member died October 26, 1874.[36] Typhoid reappeared in Fort Walsh in the summer of 1876 (one case) and in the hospital cases registered for 1877 (several mild cases). In 1878 he said there were eleven cases, three he classified as Typhoid-Malarial. In 1879 there were seventeen cases of which one was classified as Typhoid-Malarial.

In 1878 Kittson searched for the cause and method of transmission for the typhoid cases. He believed transmission was by water and not by air, and from contaminated swamps in the Cypress Hills, which contained decomposing vegetable matter and carcasses of horses and buffalo. In rainy weather, the marshes overflowed and the excess water spilled into the nearby creek. A few days later the first case of "Mountain Fever" of Typhoid-Malarial description broke out amongst the settlers. Out of five half-breed hamlets in the Hills only one escaped the epidemic. It was in a secluded spot in a beautiful forest fed by a clear spring water.

Kittson found a cesspool out behind the Division A huts at Fort Walsh. It had become contaminated by the Sergeant's mess cook throwing kitchen slop into it. The men complained of a bad smell coming up from underneath the floor of their nearby bunkroom. To prevent an outbreak, the men were quarantined outside the Fort and a separate latrine tent was pitched. Huts were disinfected with the fumes of burning sulfur on a rotation basis. Windows were inserted to improve ventilation. Bunks were replaced with wooden beds. Cesspools were drained or eradicated and men were moved into the more spacious Quarter Master's building. A new water well was dug nearby.

Above: Assistant NWMP Commissioner James F. Macleod, ca1876-80.
Glenbow Archives NA-23-2

Below: Sketched by R.B. Nevitt, *Fort Macleod*, 1875.
Collection of Glenbow Museum, Calgary, Canada

Fort Macleod Dec. 1874.

The treatment of the day for typhoid was to give quinine in large doses, within the first forty-eight hours of the first symptoms. Opium was given for the diarrhea. Drs. Kittson and Jukes called the treatment the only hope, but invariably successful if administered early.[37]

Thirty-five percent of the diseases recorded by Kittson in his 1879 report were of an infectious nature. The improved hygiene practices resulted in only one case of fever in Fort Walsh. The victim had contracted the disease outside the Fort. Dr. Kittson recommended seven sanitary measures and supported an eighth, Dr. Kennedy's request for separate lavatories, for all NWMP Forts.

Dr. Kittson noted two other interesting Indian cases. Both were "lunatics". One was an old squaw, who with kind treatment and good food recovered. The second was a young half-breed, who had endangered his nephews but was found to be perfectly harmless and obedient.

A case of diphtheria was diagnosed with a large accompanying abcess. Improved diets for the sick men were recommended. Kittson recommended the introduction of beer and spirits, based on his six years of experience. In total Kittson saw two hundred and thirty-five patients in 1879, which he diagnosed with neuralgia (ten), syphilis (two), chronic rheumatism (six), sore throat (thirteen), coughs etc. (twenty-one), diarrhea (fifty-three), bilious (eleven), dysentery (six), boils (four), and minor surgery (thirty-four). The average stay in the hospital was ten days. His average hospital census was about seven and sick parade attendance one to two men each day.

The 1879 Report of Dr. George A. Kennedy

In Surgeon Kennedy's report for 1879, there were no fatalities. Two men were declared unfit for duty and invalided. Both were asthmatics, who had had their disease before they joined the Force. One had been getting worse for five years while in the NWMP. The other had the disease for eight years and was told the dryness of the country was excellent for asthmatics. He too had worsened since his arrival. Kennedy concluded it was not a place for asthmatics and recommended examining physicians be so cautioned.

On September 20, 1879 Surgeon Kittson developed remitting or Mountain-Fever, while treating Inspector Steele at Fort Walsh. Surgeon Kennedy was called to Fort Walsh. Sergeant John Lauder replaced Kennedy at Fort Macleod. On Dr. Kennedy's arrival at Fort Walsh, there were another sixty fever (non-NWMP) cases to treat.

Kennedy also treated a large number of Indians, chiefly Bloods, Blackfeet and North Peigans that year. The commonest Indian diseases involved eye infections and chest infections, which he observed were particularly common amongst females. Most females over the age of thirty did not have "sound lungs".

After making recommendations to improve hygiene, Kennedy asked that a new hospital be built at Fort Walsh, and declared that the current one was unfit for habitation. He noted a half-inch of dust everywhere in summer, an inability to keep the hospital warm in the winter and the possibility that the roof was falling down. He saw two hundred and six patients with an average of six a day at his clinic. The average length of stay in hospital was extended because of the two asthmatics.

1878-1929 Dr. Nevitt's Post NWMP Years

Dr. Nevitt never met his successor, Dr. G.A. Kennedy, the fourth NWMP Surgeon. Nevitt returned to Toronto on June 22, 1878 and took the hand of Elizabeth (Lizzy) Beaty, his fiancée of four years, to whom he had written so many descriptive letters. The 145 Nevitt letters were written from October 1874 to June 1875. They were acquired in 1974 by Glenbow Foundation of Calgary from Nevitt's grand daughter Mrs. A.A. McArthur of Hamilton, Ontario, along with many sketches and watercolours.[38]

In October 1878, Dr. Nevitt recommenced his medical studies. He completed the requirements for an MD from Trinity Medical College in 1882, after which he took a special course in Obstetrics and Gynecology in London, England.[39]

In 1883 he was appointed as the "Chair of Sanitary Science" at Women's Medical College (WMC). When an unexpected death occurred and the Professor of Surgery position opened in 1887, Dr. Richard Barrington Nevitt was appointed the WMC Head of Surgery and managed all the surgical departments except Obstetrics and Gynecology.

In 1888 Nevitt succeeded Dr. Alexander McPhedran as the Dean of the Women's Medical College. He held that position until it federated with the Trinity Medical College and the University of Toronto in 1906. Dr. Nevitt stopped teaching at that time, but remained a member of the Academy of Medicine of which he was one of the founders. The Academy made him an honourary member shortly before his death in 1928.

Dr. Nevitt was described by colleagues as tall and distinguished, as having a good clinical instinct, a trained mind and a deft hand. He was "modest and retiring, strong in will and inflexible in purpose". He averaged a baby delivery a day throughout his career.[40] He had a scholarly interest in Greek and Roman authors. On one occasion he translated a German medical book into English. His knowledge of Latin was functional as well.[41]

Dr. Nevitt as an Early Artist

In addition to his medical and obstetrical skills, Dr. Nevitt honed his sketching skills while out west. He was a natural artist, although he was never formally trained. He made a point of capturing all the major events that he attended. A total of 107 sketches were acquired by Glenbow Foundation of Calgary in the NWMP Trek's centennial year, 1974. Seventy-six were put on exhibit, along with ten more that were loaned from the Art Gallery of Hamilton, Ontario.[42]

Nevitt wasn't the only artist on the 1874 March. Twenty-two year old artist Henri Julien was sent by the Canadian Illustrated News with the second contingent that left Toronto on June 6, 1874. Julien completed forty sketches, which were printed in the News.[43]

The Nevitts had Six Children

The Nevitts had two daughters, Mary, the wife of Edgerton Ryerson, an Anglican Minister, and Sarah the wife of Dr. Davidson Black the anatomist, who discovered the Peking skeletons (Homo Siniensis) in China. Two sons died in WWI: - Reverend Barrington Nevitt in 1918, and Bertram, who was killed in action in 1916. The two surviving sons were Irving and Richard of Toronto. Elizabeth Nevitt died in 1927, nine months before Dr. Richard Barrington Nevitt passed away on May 11, 1928. He was buried in Toronto.

Upper sketch - R.B. Nevitt, *First Whiskey Spilled*, 1874,
Collection of Glenbow Museum, Calgary, Canada.

Lower Sketch - R.B. Nevitt, *The Forge Fort Macleod*, 1875.
Collection of Glenbow Museum, Calgary, Canada.

Dr. George Allan Kennedy, MB
1858-1913

*"Contemptuous of a cloistered sheltered life,
(He)...Spurned the tedium of the trodden ways;
Eager to blaze new trails through lands unknown,
To trace new trails across the foaming Sea,
Eager to sow where others had not sown,
Eager to challenge unknown Destiny"![1]*

Glenbow Archives NA-2227-1

Introduction

Dr. George A. Kennedy was the first full-time physician to arrive in the NWT and stay for the remainder of his life.[2] He came to Fort Macleod in 1878 as a NWMP surgeon, while still a twenty-year old. His University of Toronto (UofT) Dean of Medicine had referred him to the NWMP, because he was too young to practice or likely legally sign his prescriptions. And he loved the outdoors.

During Dr. Kennedy's eight years with the NWMP 1878-1887, he carefully observed and succinctly described medicine on the Canadian frontier.[3] His annual medical reports are the most explicit, informative and consistently well told summaries of the diseases the NWMP surgeons treated; the diagnoses they made; and the hygiene measures they introduced, during that era. But it was not straightforward medicine. Having to treat the twenty-nine hundred Sioux, that came into Canada with Sitting Bull from 1876-1881, provided a high risk diversion from the mundane life of daily NWMP sick parades. Unfortunately when it came to treatment, Kennedy had the most frugal of drug cupboards.

The fact that he stayed, renewed his NWMP contract, settled in Fort Macleod, the town that grew up around the NWMP Fort, and remained a prairie medical leader for thirty-five years, attests to the depth of his calling and the medical competence he brought to it. His colleagues could always call upon him, and did, as the medical organizations in the NWT and Alberta were formed. Dr. Kennedy was in the vanguard that brought full-time physicians to the prairies, built the hospitals, introduced medicine, surgery, good hygiene practices, and set the professional example to be followed.

On his arrival in Fort Macleod in October 1878, Dr. Kennedy became responsible for a 22,500 square mile tract of land in southern Alberta along the 49th parallel. A year after his arrival he faced his first outbreak of "typhomalaria or remitting" fever and had to treat over sixty cases, including two of his own superiors at Fort Walsh in the Cypress Hills.

Despite being politically thwarted from being appointed as the senior NWMP surgeon in 1882 at age twenty-three, Dr. Kennedy decided to remain in the Force and did so for another five years. He strove to improve hospital facilities, sanitation and hygiene in and around the Forts. Concerned at the inability to control the unremitting fever that closed Fort Walsh in 1882, he made a second research proposal to systematically study the fever problem at all Forts in 1886. His superior, Dr. Augustus Jukes did not support the request. Yet this fever would cause twenty-three of ninety-six NWMP deaths from 1886-1900 alone, the commonest of any fatal disease

Kennedy carefully recorded his own observations and presented his research on the subject at the first Canadian Medical Association (CMA) meeting west of Toronto held in Banff in 1889. It was the first medical paper in the NWT. At the same meeting Dr. R.G Brett who was elected the CMA Vice-President for the NWT, succeeded Dr. A. Jukes. The next day Dr. Kennedy became the first President of the newly formed North West Territories Medical Association (NWTMA). By the late 1890's the cause of the serious fever that plagued the NWMP Forts was known to be typhoid fever. In 1904/5 a NWT medical laboratory was built in Regina, at the insistence of the NWT Medical Council Executive.[4]

Having made the decision to remain in Fort Macleod for the rest of his life, Kennedy retired from the Force in 1887. He had already established a private practice and started the Macleod Gazette newspaper in 1882. He married in 1883, started a family 1884, built a home 1885, and would help to build many early institutions in Fort Macleod.

When the NWT became the Provinces of Saskatchewan and Alberta in 1905, Dr. Kennedy was one of the medical leaders who helped form the Alberta Medical Association (AMA) and College of Physicians and Surgeons of Alberta. In recognition, Kennedy was made the first honourary President of the College of Physicians and Surgeons of Alberta in 1906, and was elected the second President in 1907.

Along with Dr. R.G. Brett, Dr. Kennedy sought to resolve the problem created by diversely trained physicians moving their practices to the prairies. The migration led to the creation of the NWT medical registration system in 1885 and NWT College in 1888 to examine, license, and register new physicians. Drs. Kennedy and Brett proposed the formation of a Western Canadian Medical Federation in 1907, to reciprocally register physicians in the four western provinces. By taking the initiative and presenting the proposal at the CMA convention in Winnipeg in 1909, they were able to move the stalemated discussions for a national licensing body forward. To pass the Canada Medical or "Roddick" Act by 1912[5] required the unanimous approval of all provincial medical associations and legislatures, the CMA and Canadian House of Commons. Kennedy unexpectedly died the next year.

1858-1878   From Youth to Bachelor of Medicine (MB)

George Allan Kennedy was born in Dundas, Ontario on April 16, 1858. He was raised in a strict Presbyterian household. As a youth he came to love the outdoors and Mother Nature. He would find injured birds or animals and take them home and treat their injuries or set their fractures.

Dundas was the Ontario town where Dr. William Osler had grown up and left nine years before, to study medicine at the University of Toronto. He too loved nature and the outdoors. The two likely knew each other as Osler did four preceptorships or locums in Dundas and Hamilton from 1868-1874, when Kennedy was 10-16 years of age. Osler had finished his medical degree in Montreal in 1872 and joined the McGill Medical Faculty in 1874. Quite possibly Osler was one of Kennedy's role models.[6]

After graduating from St. Catharines Collegiate circa 1873,[7] Kennedy headed to UofT to follow his dream of a career in medicine. Graduating as the silver medallist in his class of 1878, he interned at the Hamilton General Hospital. Six months later, and not yet twenty-one, Dr. Kennedy was still too young to enter medical practice. The UofT Dean of Medicine recommended him to replace Dr. R.B. Nevitt as the fourth NWMP surgeon. Like his predecessors Drs. Kittson, Nevitt and R. Miller,[8] he received a salary of $1000 per year. His contract commenced on Oct 2, 1878.

Heading west from Toronto on the Great Western and Union Pacific Railways, Kennedy boarded the sternwheeler "Missouri Queen" in St. Louis. The next six days were spent either on a sand bar or on the Missouri River, dialoguing with one of the two hundred and fifty passengers onboard, the well known author Mark Twain (Samuel Clemens).[9] Twain was on a contract from the American Government to lecture new settlers on their civic responsibilities. Kennedy stayed another three days to listen to Twain's speeches to new settlers in Fort Benton and Helena, Montana. Then he headed to Canadian NWT with the latest batch of fifteen to twenty new NWMP personnel, enjoying a taste of his first Indian summer. Following the riverside chats with Twain, Kennedy described his future work in a letter to his parents. He said he would seek to "bring relief to the suffering, and introduce preventive medicine to whites, Indians and members of the Force alike".[10]

1878-1887   The NWMP Years

Dr. Kennedy arrived at Fort Macleod in October 1878. He was the sole practitioner for a practice that stretched 150 miles from the Rocky Mountains, to near the Saskatchewan border and northward 150 miles from the American border to halfway between Fort Macleod and Calgary. His practice at first included the Blood and Peigan Reserves at Cardston and Gleichen; one hundred NWMP Officers, another one hundred townspeople, and nearby settlers. The Indian Reservations harboured many social problems, which Kennedy foresaw would be exacerbated by the loss of the buffalo. The buffalo would be gone by 1879.[11]

Kennedy's first major medical problem was "typhomalaria fever". The infamous fever went under numerous titles: Rocky Mountain Fever, Red River Fever, typhomalaria or typhomastic fever and remitting fever. He concluded it was caused by malaria because its clinical presentation was inconsistent, its severity was unpredictable and it responded to quinine. The severe cases he felt were because typhoid fever was superimposed on the malaria. The combined effect he noted, increased morbidity and mortality. He didn't believe the two entities were from the same source.

In the fall of 1879 Dr. Kennedy was called to Fort Walsh from Fort Macleod. There he found over sixty cases of "fever" waiting for him. One case involved his Chief, Dr. John Kittson,[12] who had become infected for a second time. The first was in 1874. Kittson became ill after treating another case, NWMP Inspector (later Sir) Sam Steele. Fortunately both survived, although barely. To Dr. Kennedy the harsh reality was that the hygiene of Fort Walsh and its location in a draw was particularly unsatisfactory.[13] He undertook to improve the physical structure, the placement of privies, etc. and left orders to enforce his recommendations.

It was some months before officers Steele or Kittson were able to resume their duties. Kittson's incapacity left Dr. Kennedy attending and treating the twenty-nine hundred Sioux that had accompanied Sitting Bull in the Cypress Hills, when they escaped over the Canadian border, following the defeat of General Custer at the Battle of the Little Big Horn in 1876. The nearest

Fort to care for and treat the Sioux was Wood Mountain, which was another one hundred miles east of Fort Walsh.

In his annual NWMP Report, covering 1880[14] Dr. Kennedy wrote about treating the diarrhea and dysentery that spread so easily through the Indian camps; as well as the measles, whooping cough and influenza. He enumerated the usual waves of smallpox, winter frostbites, accidents, trauma and gunshot injuries, amongst the 200-400 men that were annually admitted to the Fort Walsh hospital. The manpower at the Fort was less than half that number. The daily sick parades he noted, averaged about 8% of the total NWMP strength.[15]

In 1881 syphilis and gonorrhea arrived from south of the border. The two venereal diseases infected not only the Indians, but also about twenty recruits at Fort Walsh.[16] To everyone's relief, that same year the remnants of the Sioux Band returned to the United States.

Dr. John Kittson resigned in 1881. On January 1, 1882 Dr. Augustus Jukes from St. Catharines was appointed the NWMP senior surgeon, by Prime Minister Sir John A. Macdonald. Dr. Kennedy was placed in charge of Forts Macleod and Calgary, in the renamed Western Division of the NWMP. Jukes did not arrive until the summer of 1882. In January and February of 1882 Kennedy faced a smallpox epidemic alone. He vaccinated 150-200 Indian children along the US border. The uptake from the vaccinations was seventy percent. His efforts aborted the epidemic at the border.

Six months later, on July 30, 1882, Kennedy was joined by Staff Sergeant Dr. Leverett George deVeber, whom he stationed in Calgary, replacing "Doc" John Lauder who had resigned.[17]

Kennedy had concluded by 1882 that try as he might, Fort Walsh could not be cleaned up.[18] The problem was water-based and no matter how much attention was paid to hygiene, the fever still remained endemic. With the arrival of the CPR in Regina in 1882, Fort Walsh was closed and Surgeon Jukes' headquarters were moved to Regina.

In the summer of 1883 Kennedy arranged for temporary medical coverage at Macleod (deVeber), and Calgary (Henderson). He was pleased when Dr. F.X. Girard of Montreal arrived. Girard was the first physician assigned to the Blood and Peigan Reservations and would stay from 1883-1900.[19] Coupled with medical coverage from Regina by Dr. Jukes, Dr. Kennedy was free to board the CPR which had reached Calgary on August 11, 1883 and take a passenger train to Ontario. There he married Alice Maude Allen, whom he had met when she first visited her brother at Fort Walsh in 1881.[20]

The Kennedys returned to Calgary on January 2, 1884, in time for Dr. Kennedy to approve the renovations that he had proposed for the hospital at Fort Calgary. Then he traveled to Fort Macleod to supervise the new hospital that was being constructed there. It was finished by May 20 of 1884 and contained the first Operating Room (OR) in the NWT. Kennedy said the hospital was probably the best in the prairie west.[21]

Above: The Fort Macleod hospital as it appeared in late 1800's.
University of Alberta Archives (Jamieson collection) 75-112-30-14

Earlier in 1884 Kennedy had been advertising for a druggist to join him. He was successful in May 1884 in securing Mr. J.D. Higinbotham, a nineteen year old pharmacist from Ontario.[22] Unfortunately unrest was building on the prairies. Changes in the land survey system, from the river based lots to the grid system, were having an unsettling effect on the Metis. It was a repetition of what had occurred in Manitoba in 1869/70. In 1884 the Metis convinced Louis Riel to come back from Montana to lead their protest movement. Riel's confrontational approach with the Federal Government eventually led to the forty-seven day second Riel or Northwest Rebellion from March 26 to May 12, 1885.

Kennedy did not join the militia. He remained the only physician at Fort Macleod, when Dr. L.G. deVeber enlisted in the Rocky Mountain Rangers. A rumor of warring Indians nearby led to the formation of a summer search patrol, which Kennedy joined. The patrol scoured the countryside but found no traces of the rumored Indians.[23]

In the fall of 1885 Kennedy diagnosed his first case of scarlet fever. He described the case in the English medical literature.[24] He also completed construction of his first home in January of that year.[25] At yearend Dr. Kennedy's wife, Alice, who had moved east in April at the start of the Rebellion, returned in time to deliver their son Alan in December.

In October 1885 his druggist Mr. J.D. Higinbotham, encouraged by the rapid expansion of the coal mining community, moved to Lethbridge. For the next two months Higinbotham, Kennedy and deVeber practiced "medicine by mail...without sentencing anyone to the cemetery".[26] It appears that Kennedy owned the building in Lethbridge in which Higinbotham opened his drugstore, just as he had in Fort Macleod.[27] Both Drs. deVeber and Kennedy made frequent trips to Lethbridge as it had no physician. In December 1885 the Galt Coal Mining Company and the NWMP offered Dr. F.H. Mewburn, the house Surgeon at the Winnipeg General

Hospital, a mine and police contract and the promise of a new three bed hospital. He came to Lethbridge in January 1886.

Drs. Mewburn and Kennedy were of similar minds. Both were bright, forthright, aggressive, surgically-audacious, competent and medically well read.[28] Six months after Mewburn's 1886 arrival, the two had an unexpected summer visitor, Dr. William Osler, who at that time was the Professor of Medicine in Philadelphia. Dr. Osler was accompanied by his brother Edmund and four other businessmen, on the four week CPR Transcontinental trip in August 1886.[29] Details about the trip are sketchy and inferential. One impact was probably on Kennedy's December 1886 NWMP report. He re-proposed his fever research project to determine the frequency, severity and characteristics of the fever at each Fort. The Osler meeting may also have been the stimulus for Kennedy's research of cow (or buffalo) milk as a tuberculosis vector, that he noted in his 1890 NWTMA report.[30] Unfortunately Dr. A. Jukes didn't support the fever research request, so individual Forts failed to benefit from any standard definition or reporting of their cases. The question of whether the fever was typhoid or malaria continued to vex Kennedy for a decade.[31]

After Dr. F.H. Mewburn's arrival in 1886, Mewburn and Kennedy undertook more sophisticated surgical challenges. Dr. Leverett George deVeber periodically supported them as the anesthetist.[32] Originally the surgery was done in Fort Macleod, as Dr. Mewburn did not have an OR and would not get one until 1891.

In 1887 an order came from the new NWMP Commissioner Herchmer transferring Dr. Kennedy to North Battleford. Kennedy declined the move and instead entered full-time private practice in Fort Macleod on June 30, 1887.

1887-1905 Private Practice in the NWT

By 1887, Dr. Kennedy had already demonstrated his competence at treating orthopedic fractures and gun-shot wounds. But he faced a major challenge when his friend, lawyer C.C. McCaul accidentally shot himself in the chest on June 23, 1887.[33] The bullet entered the top of the rib cage, slightly to the right of the mid-line and came out through the shoulder blade in the back. It missed the major vessels of the heart. Kennedy treated McCaul conservatively, until there were localized signs of a pleural effusion and pus in the chest. Dr. F.H. Mewburn came to Fort Macleod and operated on Mr. McCaul, exploring the bullet entrance site. It became a sucking wound and almost killed McCaul. In a second operation Mewburn removed parts of two ribs underneath the right armpit. The chest cavity was washed and drains were left in place. Postoperatively the dressings were changed "by the bed sheet". McCaul survived.[34] Fortunately he did, for it was McCaul's meteorological data that Kennedy used to reach his conclusions in his 1889 CMA convention paper.[35]

The twenty-second annual Canadian Medical Association (CMA) Meeting was held in Banff August 12-13, 1889.[36] It was the first CMA meeting west of Toronto. Dr. Kennedy's presentation on "The Climate of Southern Alberta and its Relation to Health and Disease" concluded that the health in Southern Albertans was "better" because of the late onset of winter, the Chinooks, the reduced temperature fluctuation and the warmer weather. He supported his conclusions by noting the prairies lacked tuberculosis or pneumonia and he rarely saw any rheumatism or "malaria" (mountain or remitting fever) except in and around the Forts. The concept, and controversy surrounding it, reverberated for years.[37]

The 1889 CMA convention agenda was overloaded with eighteen papers from the eighty-nine participants.[38] Kennedy's paper was the first to be presented by a prairie physician. Dr. A. Jukes was also at the convention and planned to present his paper on "The Endemic Fever in the NWT". When Jukes' paper was "rescheduled from first to last" on the slate, he withdrew it. Fortunately both papers were subsequently published in the Northern Lancet Supplement (Jukes)[39] and the Montreal Medical Journal (Kennedy).[40] They clearly disagreed on the cause and etiology of the prairie prevalent fever. Kennedy stressed personal hygiene along with treatment; Jukes ordered high doses of quinine. Years later Dr. R.B. Deane, who knew and respected both Drs. Kennedy and Jukes, said he could never understand Dr. Jukes' obsession with calling the fever malaria. He reiterated the great respect he had for Dr. Jukes' ability and knowledge, "except on this occasion".[41]

H.C. Jamieson quotes "others" as saying that Dr. Kennedy had not only become an enthusiast for the West by 1889, but had lost his sense of judgment.[42] That didn't stop eastern physicians from giving Kennedy multiple offers to return east. He declined them all.

In 1890 Dr. Kennedy read an article in the French medical literature suggesting that bone chips from the leg of a dog could be used to treat human fractures that didn't unite. He and Dr. F.H. Mewburn tried the dog bone approach on NWMP Cst. W.W. Phillips on November 15, 1890 in Fort Macleod. The chips were rejected. Drs. Kennedy and Mewburn re-operated on Phillips in Lethbridge on February 6, 1891. The leg had to be shortened two inches. Constable Phillips lived until 1944.[43] One year later it was reported in the literature that the French approach would not work.[44]

Two memorable stories have been handed down from Dr. Kennedy's operations with Dr. Mewburn.[45] One was a hernia repair. It involved an eighty-year old Priest. The operation was performed using a spinal anesthetic, with the Bishop comforting the Priest. A fly came into the OR and Dr. Mewburn blew up. "Kennedy kill that fly or put the Bishop out. I don't give a damn which, as I can't hold myself any longer". On another OR day Dr. Mewburn was concerned over the patient's pupil size. It was small and pinpointed. He thought the patient had been given too much anesthetic and told Dr. Kennedy. Kennedy replied, "Hell, that's his glass eye".

NWT Medical Association

Dr. Kennedy was always on call for requests to advance the organization and practice of medicine. His first challenge came in 1889, when he was elected President of the Northwest Territories Medical Association, at the organizational meeting after the Banff CMA convention. Shortly afterwards, Dr. R.G. Brett of Banff was elected head of the new NWT Medical Executive Council, the body responsible for the College functions including examinations and registration. Brett also became the CMA Vice-President for the NWT that year, succeeding Dr. Jukes.

At the second NWT Medical Association meeting in Medicine Hat in 1890, Dr. Kennedy spoke eloquently to the members and predicted "...from small acorns, giant oaks will grow....I have an idea we are not formed of the stuff of which failures are made. Our highest duty is to prevent disease, to act as guardians of the public health, to keep the enemy always on the outside".[46]

Although Dr. Kennedy retired from the NWMP in 1887, he was periodically asked to fill in when there were no NWMP Surgeons available. Concerned about the future of the NWMP hospital in Fort Macleod, he helped incorporate an Auxiliary to build a new hospital. It would be a further nine years before one was required and built. After the CPR Railway was extended from Fort Macleod to Edmonton in 1892, Drs. Kennedy and Brett often traveled to Calgary to assist Dr. H.G. Mackid with their surgery.[47]

Dr. Kennedy was appointed the Inspector of Hospitals by the NWT Legislative Assembly from 1897-1905. It required him to visit, inspect and approve hospitals that requested legislative grants from the Assembly. It was an early form of accreditation.[48]

In 1901 Dr. Kennedy became alarmed at the inadequate medical services that were being provided by the Federal Government to the nearby Indian Reserves. Dr. Girard had recently left. He petitioned the Minister of the Interior, Clifford Sifton for assistance.[49] Later that year the respected Dr. O.C. Edwards accepted the call to provide medical care. Edwards returned to the west and the Blood Indian Reserves of Southern Alberta as the second full time physician. Shortly after Edwards arrival, he participated in the signing of Treaty #8 in Northern Alberta.[50] Dr. Edwards lived weekdays at Standoff on the Blood Reserve and weekends in Fort Macleod, for the next fifteen years. After his death in 1915, his wife, Henrietta Muir Edwards became recognized for her research of women's issues. She was one of the five ladies, later known as the "Five Persons", who made their famous appeal to the Canadian Supreme Court and Privy Council in 1927-29 so women would be recognized as "persons".

On April 29, 1903 at 4:10 AM Turtle Mountain fractured, causing the Frank Slide. Drs. Kennedy and Edwards assembled their own nursing team and traveled to Frank, early on the morning of April 30. Fortunately the swath of rock had spared ninety percent of the town. About seventy people were killed or buried and four were seriously injured. Dr. George Malcolmson had already converted his house and annex into a hospital for those that needed medical care. Since nothing more could be accomplished medically, the team returned the next day to Fort Macleod.[51]

Below: Members of the first Medical Council of Canada, Nov 7-9, 1912. Most doctors are not identified. Back row within the ogive stands Dr. George A. Kennedy, Second last man on the right rear row is Dr. R. G. Brett and fourth man from the left in the front row is Dr. Thomas Roddick.

From the History of the Medical Council of Canada

1905-1913 Private Practice in Alberta

Dr. Kennedy was elected President of the NWT College of Physicians and Surgeons from 1902/06.[52] On September 1, 1905 Alberta and Saskatchewan became provinces. At the inaugural March 6, 1906 meeting, Dr. Kennedy made the motion to establish the Alberta Medical Association (AMA). The Alberta Medical Profession Act was passed at the first sitting of the Alberta Government legislature in May 1906. It established the Alberta College of Physicians and Surgeons and outlined the responsibilities of the AMA. In 1906/07 Dr. Brett was elected the first President of both the College and the Association. Dr. Kennedy was named the 1906/7 Honourary President of the Alberta College. At the 1907 meeting, Dr. Kennedy became the second President of the College.[53]

Mindful of the difficulties that followed from setting annual examinations for new physicians, Dr. Kennedy took the initiative as the "western" Roddick to re-raise the long-standing issue of a national Canadian medical examination in late 1908.[54] He again proposed that a common exam and reciprocal registration system be established amongst the four western provinces, through formation of the Western Canadian Medical Federation. Dr. R.G. Brett joined the initiative, as did two leading physicians from Manitoba, Drs. T.N. Milroy and James Patterson.[55] After visiting physicians in Regina and Vancouver, the western physicians managed to put the subject back on the August 23-25, 1909 CMA Convention Agenda in Winnipeg. All four prairie medical associations supported it. The revisit was successful in securing approval for a CMA committee to meet with Dr. Thomas Roddick, the architect of the national examination system. By 1912 the Canadian Medical (Roddick) Act was passed by every provincial Medical Association, Provincial Legislature, the CMA and the House of Commons. It created the Dominion Medical Council of Canada (MCC), which has continued to examine physicians ever since.

The Medical Council of Canada (MCC) sets a voluntary examination and issues a certificate, Licence of the Medical Council of Canada (LMCC) to successful physicians. LMCCs are recognized throughout Canada for provincial registration.[56]

Below: Members of the NWT/Alberta Medical Association executive ca1905. Rear L to R - Dr. J.D. Lafferty, Calgary; Dr. George Kennedy, Fort Macleod; Dr. A.B. Stewart?, Rosthern. Front L to R - Dr. T.H. Whitelaw, Edmonton and Dr. R.G. Brett, Banff.　　　　　Glenbow Archives NA-791-1

Dr. Kennedy was briefly involved in the establishment of the University of Alberta (UofA). He became a member of the first UofA Senate in 1908. He resigned shortly afterwards possibly because of his 1909 Western Canadian Medical Federation commitments.[57]

Fort Macleod Community Contributions

Dr. Kennedy not only had considerable medical skills, but he also had a wide variety of avocational interests.[58] When the first Fort Macleod Historical Society was formed in December 1884, members were looking for subjects to present. Kennedy began to research the famous 1870 Battle of Belly River. It was the last major battle between the Crees and Blackfoot. The battle occurred underneath the site of the future CPR High Level Bridge at Lethbridge. Kennedy interviewed Jerry Potts, who had participated in it. Then he asked surveyor Charles A. Magrath to make a sketch of the battle scene. He summarized his research in the Lethbridge News on April 30, 1890.[59] Along with C.E.D. (later Judge) Wood, Kennedy started the Macleod Gazette newspaper on June 1, 1882. When it became too conservative, he and two colleagues started the short lived Macleod Outlaw newspaper in 1896.

Below Players from the 1894 Macleod polo team. Left to right - William Humphrey, Albert Browning, Michael Holland, George A. Kennedy.
　　　　　　　　　　　　　　　　　　　　Glenbow Archives NA-460-4

Dr. Kennedy sat on many Fort Macleod Boards, including the Board of Trade in 1888, the School Board in 1894, and the Hospital Board as its secretary in 1889. He also chaired the North West Territories Committee on Public Health and Preventive Medicine. Although he was a good friend and colleague of lawyer and later NWT Legislative "Premier" (Sir) Frederick Haultain, Kennedy never entered politics. Instead he helped initiate the Macleod Turf Association in 1889, the Fort Macleod Debating Society about 1890, the Polo Club in 1891 and the Fort Macleod Golf Course 1890. The latter two were "firsts" west of Winnipeg.[60] He actively participated in the building of the first and second Fort Macleod public hospitals in 1893 and 1911/12.

In September 1937, his son Dr. Alan Kennedy donated the Kennedy Golf Trophy for medal play at the annual provincial medical golf tournament, in his father's memory. Dr. G.A. Kennedy was an excellent marksman and horseman. But when Dr. L.G. deVeber caught him shooting an antelope out of season, it led to a tense touché. The two laughed it off and Kennedy paid the twenty-five dollar fine.[61]

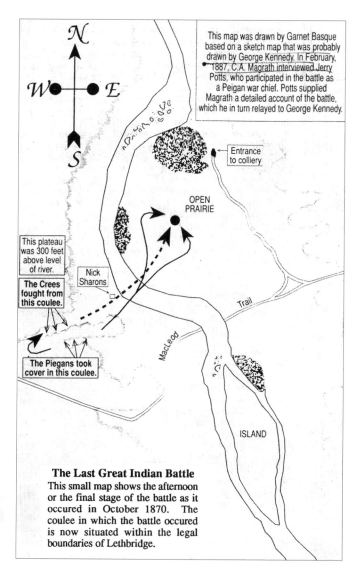

This map was drawn by Garnet Basque based on a sketch map that was probably drawn by George Kennedy. In February, 1887, C.A. Magrath interviewed Jerry Potts, who participated in the battle as a Peigan war chief. Potts supplied Magrath a detailed account of the battle, which he in turn relayed to George Kennedy.

N

W E

S

Entrance to colliery

OPEN PRAIRIE

This plateau was 300 feet above level of river.

Nick Sharons

Trail

The Crees fought from this coulee.

The Piegans took cover in this coulee.

Macleod

ISLAND

The Last Great Indian Battle

This small map shows the afternoon or the final stage of the battle as it occured in October 1870. The coulee in which the battle occured is now situated within the legal boundaries of Lethbridge.

Above - Re sketched from a map probably drawn by Dr. George Kennedy in February 1887 while he and Charles A. Magrath discussed the famous last battle.

Dr. R. Lampard collection

Dr. Kennedy and Family

Dr. G.E. Learmonth met Dr. Kennedy in 1903 and described him as the epitome of a NWMP officer. He was "of medium height, of handsome features and of military bearing. I was much attracted by his genial personality and keen intelligence".[62]

Dr. F.H. Mewburn remembered Dr. Kennedy in a speech in 1928, as a physician who lived the "...mode of ordinary everyday life and all that went with it....He always lived up to it, never faltered, never broke faith with his fellows. With his optimism, his imagination, his patriotism, his imperialism in the widest sense of the term...Kennedy will take his place with those men who in the early and succeeding days, under stress and strain and many difficulties, laid the foundation, materially and intellectually, of the life we are enjoying today".[63]

The Kennedys were blessed with two children, a daughter Ethel Francis born in 1884 and a son Alan born in 1885. Alan entered medicine at McGill.[64] After graduation he undertook post-graduate studies in the management and treatment of tuberculosis, in Europe

and at Johns Hopkins Hospital in Baltimore, Maryland U.S.A., before returning to Fort Macleod in 1908 to join his father in practice. Alan lived and practiced in Fort Macleod until he passed away in 1954. Alan's return allowed Dr. G.A. Kennedy Sr. to plan a similar sabbatical to study tuberculosis treatment in England. Unfortunately the clock was ticking for Dr. George Allan Kennedy. In March of 1913 he discovered he had an ulcer on his tongue that wouldn't heal. It progressed and was diagnosed as cancerous.[65] He sought the advice of his colleagues in Lethbridge, Edmonton, and Winnipeg. Treatment in Winnipeg was unsuccessful and he died there on October 8, 1913.[66]

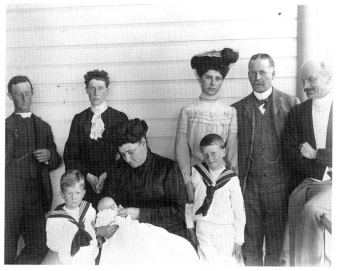

Above: Group of St. Paul's Anglican Mission to the Blood Indian Reserve, ca1898-1903. Left to right - Rev. Arthur de B. Owens; Mrs. Arthur Owens; Mrs. George A. Kennedy; D.J. Campbell's baby; Kenny Kennedy; Mrs. ? Ward; Dr. George A. Kennedy; D.J. Campbell. Glenbow Archives NA-670-25

Dr. George A. Kennedy's death was most untimely. He had just been named, along with Dr. Thomas Roddick, as one of the three federal cabinet appointees, to the first Board of the Dominion Medical Council of Canada. Dr. Kennedy joined Drs. R.G. Brett and John Park on the Board as Alberta's 1912 representatives.[67]

The Kennedy funeral was the largest in Fort Macleod's history. Interment was in the Macleod Cemetery. A plaque was later placed in the Fort Macleod Anglican Church, to commemorate the life and work of Dr. George Allan Kennedy.[68]

If one were to look for a physician on either side of the 49th Parallel, they could find no finer example of why Natives and Whites alike, found a second reason to call that imaginary line the Medicine Line;[69] and to cross it for the medical care it offered. The name Dr. George Allan Kennedy, had become a byword amongst the Indians, where he was known far and wide as "the First White Man".

Dr. Leverett George deVeber, MD
1849-1925

*"..A square shooter, endowed with an abundance
of human kindness, always charming, courteous,
and hard working.
His word was as good as his bond."* [1]

Galt Archives GP19694786000

Introduction

Dr. Leverett George deVeber was a third generation United Empire Loyalist.[2] His great-great-grandfather Lt. Colonel Gabriel deVeber, served in the British Army during the American War of Independence.[2] After the War, Colonel deVeber received a land grant of 1000 acres south of Saint John, New Brunswick on the Musquash River.[3] The deVebers remained in the Maritimes for the next one hundred years. But Leverett George had a wanderlust. He studied medicine on two different continents, but not in Canada. His specialty became communicable diseases. His avocation was making friends, enough to enter politics in 1898 and win C.A. Magrath's vacated seat by acclamation. He was never out of politics until his death in 1925. Dr. L.G. deVeber's memory has been perpetuated through the naming of the prominent 8,494 foot high (2 589 m) Mount deVeber, visible to the west of the town of Grande Cache, north of Jasper.

1849-1870 From Youth to Bachelor of Medicine

L. George deVeber was the eldest of five children. He was born on February 10, 1849 and attended Collegiate School and the King's College in Windsor, Nova Scotia.[4] After graduation he commenced his medical studies at Harvard University in Boston. Owing to a "slight difference of opinion between him and the faculty" he remained there for only one year.[5] Then he transferred to the St. Bartholomew's Medical School in London, England, where he graduated with his medical diploma. The next year found Dr. deVeber in the United States, where he studied for another year at the University of Pennsylvania. In 1870 he received his degree in medicine.[6] On graduation he was immediately "commandeered into service" to help treat patients in the severe epidemic of smallpox in Philadelphia. That outbreak occurred in the same year as the second worst smallpox outbreak on the prairies, the epidemic of 1869/70. Dr. deVeber remained an authority on smallpox the rest of his life.[7] It also stimulated his lifelong interest in public health.

1871-1882 The New Brunswick years

After his term in Philadelphia, Dr. deVeber returned to Saint John, New Brunswick, where he practiced for the next decade.[8] Dr. deVeber loved the outdoors. He approached mother nature with considerable natural athletic ability. He excelled at many sports: cricket, rowing, shooting and hunting. deVeber once rowed in a practice race against Canadian Rowing Olympian Edward Hanlon of St. Catharines. He was beaten but "not outdistanced". His splendid physique, with his wide shoulders and slim hips accentuated his presence. As one colleague said, he was "an exponent of the most advanced standards of manhood". Nor was he beyond using these attributes with "telling effect".[9]

1882-1885 NWMP years

At some stage in his youthful life, he took up horsemanship. This interest and his love of outdoor adventure, likely led him to submit his application at age 33 to join the NWMP. On May 9, 1882 he reported to Staff Sergeant (later Sir) Sam Steele in Winnipeg. He was gazetted at Winnipeg's Fort Osborne by Inspector (later Commissioner) Perry.[10] Multiple postings as a Hospital Sergeant followed. He traveled up the Assiniboine on the paddle wheeler Marquette to Fort Ellice and then over land to his first posting at Fort Qu'Appelle in 1882. Shortly afterwards he was transferred to Fort Walsh, then to Fort Macleod (July 30, 1882) and finally on November 23, 1882, he was in

Calgary serving under Captain McIlree.[11] There he replaced "Doc" John Lauder, who had resigned from the Force to become an Indian Agent. Dr. deVeber was responsible for the NWMP medical care at Fort Calgary under Dr. G.A. Kennedy of Fort Macleod.[12]

Interior of the North West Mounted Police hospital in Calgary, ca 1879. Dr. deVeber supervised this hospital from 1882 to 1885.

From: Early Medicine in Alberta

In February 1883 Dr. deVeber was transferred to Fort Macleod to replace Dr. G.A. Kennedy, who went on a sabbatical to Ontario to be married. In April a snow-blinded NWMP Constable Parker was very glad to see him in Fort Macleod.[13] In the spring of 1883, likely May, there was no physician in Calgary. Dr. Andrew Henderson would not arrive until June 9, 1883. Illness struck the Boyd family of Morley, west of Calgary and Mrs. Boyd became seriously ill. One of her boys rode to Calgary to get medical help. When he found Calgary had no doctor, the son then rode another one hundred miles to Fort Macleod! There he pleaded with Dr. deVeber to make a house call to help his mother. The boy's concern over his mother's welfare, coupled with the urgency of the story, must have convinced Dr. deVeber to go. All too often house calls were false alarms, or made too late.

Dr. deVeber borrowed four horses in succession. It took him eighteen hours to reach Morley. The last horse he secured at High River hadn't been broken. He diagnosed Mrs. Boyd as having typhoid fever. The treatment for typhoid was to use Quinine in large doses. He didn't have any. Instead he produced a small flask of brandy from his saddle pouch and offered it to Mrs. Boyd as a stimulant. She said she had never taken a drink and wouldn't start now. He opined that "she was the only tee-totaller whose opinion ever pleased him". He killed the mickie, slept the night and rode home - another 130 miles. Sadly Mrs. Boyd died several days later.[14]

Dr. deVeber remained in Fort Macleod for almost a year until Dr. Kennedy returned. The two doctors met in Calgary in January 1884, where they visited the newly renovated NWMP Calgary hospital. Dr. deVeber stayed in the bustling CPR town of Calgary as the third, but only NWMP physician. Dr. Andrew Henderson had arrived in June 1883, and was joined by Dr. Neville Lindsay, on August 14, 1883. Dr. Lindsay arrived on the second train into Clagary, three days after the first one that had carried his brother-in-law Dr. R.G. Brett.

Dr. deVeber described how civilization was slowly reaching the West. He told of "being awakened by the sound of shooting in the streets, with stray bullets splintering through the walls of the shack above his bed", and of how "he resolved the problem of safety by standing his mattress on its edge against the wall and returning to sleep in its lee".[15]

While stationed in Fort Macleod, Dr. deVeber had fallen in love with the town as well as a young lady. Dr. deVeber met Rachel Francis Ryan at an NWMP dance.[16] Rachel Ryan and Kate Horan were the only two eligible ladies in Fort Macleod and Pincher Creek. Rachel was born in Melbourne, Australia on March 19, 1862. She had already lived in New Zealand and Tasmania, before her family moved to England in 1866. Her father was in the British Army. The Ryans came to Canada in 1872 when Rachel was ten.

An independent young lady, Rachel Ryan traveled west at the age of twenty, to keep house for her brother Charles. Her trip west in 1882, took from April 1 to May 22. Charles Ryan had come west on the 1874 NWMP trek. He had retired from the Force to homestead at Pincher Creek.[17] A year later, in June 1883, Rachel's parents came to live in Fort Macleod, reuniting the Ryan family.

In January 1885 Dr. deVeber applied for discharge from the NWMP. On January 26, 1885, the Discharge Board at Fort Calgary approved "the application of NWMP #185 Constable L.G. deVeber". The cost of the pay out was $84, which was paid on February 10, 1885. It coincided with Dr. deVeber's thirty-sixth birthday.[18] Dr. and Mrs. deVeber were married later in 1885.[19]

A month before the 1885 Rebellion began, Dr. Leverett George deVeber retired from the NWMP and started the fourth full-time private practice in the North West Territories. He followed Dr. A.E. Porter in Prince Albert 1878 and Drs. L.J. Munro and H.C. Wilson in Edmonton in 1882. Dr. deVeber's practice was the first one that didn't rely on government contracts.

With the outbreak of the Northwest Rebellion on April 1, 1885, 112 men joined the newly formed Rocky Mountain Rangers under Major John O. Stewart.[20] Thirteen Rangers, including Dr. deVeber were former members of the NWMP. Dr. deVeber signed on as the Rangers regimental Surgeon. Captain Lord Richard Boyle was in charge of the Rangers #1 Troop (deVeber's Troop); ex-British Army Officer Captain Edward G. Brown commanded #2 Troop; Captain John Herron #3 Troop. Another colorful member of the Rangers was John George (Kootenai) Brown of Waterton. He galloped forty miles in one day to volunteer his twenty years of experience as a plainsman and as the Rangers Chief Scout.

The Rangers action was limited. Initially the Rangers patrolled the plains east of Medicine Hat or roughly along the Fourth meridian, where the Saskatchewan/Alberta border now lies. Their next responsibility was to protect the Foothills ranches and settlements. The last was to guard the telegraph line from Medicine Hat to Fort Macleod and the construction crews on the railway from Coal Banks (Lethbridge) to

Dunmore.[21] Scouting parties were sent to the Cypress Hills. The Rangers disbanded during the four week period from June 10 to July 8, 1885 and the men were released from service. They were paid an average of two hundred dollars each. All the Rangers received the Northwest Rebellion Canada 1885 medal.

1885-1890 The Fort Macleod years

After the militia disbanded, Dr. deVeber returned to his Fort Macleod practice. The town welcomed him back. He was already a well known and respected physician and surgeon. That fall, both Drs. Kennedy and deVeber made multiple house calls to Lethbridge, because it had no physician. Lethbridge would have no doctor, until Dr. F.H. Mewburn arrived in January 1886.[22]

Dr. deVeber's reputation for being practical with his medicinal choices was revealed in the story retold by John Kemmis. Apparently Kemmis was a patient of Dr. Rimington Mead's of Pincher Creek. He was chagrined, when Dr. Mead ordered his medicine "to be taken in drops". The supply only lasted a couple of days. So Kemmis rode seventy miles to see Dr. deVeber. Kemmis was "tickled to death" and his indigestion problem vanished, when Dr. deVeber prescribed him three quart size bottles of differently coloured medication "to be taken one tablespoon three times per day in rotation".[23]

From 1883 to 1890

Fort Macleod grew rapidly, to become one of the largest towns in the NWT. Dr. deVeber became an integral part of the community. His medical office was in Godsal House and his office hours were from 8-10 A.M., 12-2 and 6-8 P.M. He helped initiate or advance the Curling Club, the Fair Board, and the Hospital Auxiliary Board. The latter was incorporated in 1887 shortly after Dr. G.A. Kennedy left the NWMP. He was also the secretary of the Cricket Club. Early cricket memberships cost three dollars per year.[24]

In 1888 Dr. deVeber registered with the NWT Medical Council under the 1885 NWT Medical Ordinance that permitted registration on receipt of two testimonials from existing registrants.[25] No examination was required until the revised 1888 Ordinance was passed. It created the NWT College of Physicians and Surgeons, which implemented an examination and registration system in 1889.

Below - The 1891 12-15 bed Galt Hospital. Dr. Mewburn operated in the attic of this building. The original 1886 3-bed NWMP/Galt Mine Terrace Infirmary is visible at the right rear of the photo. Galt Archives GP19761721000-020

Despite many happy days in Fort Macleod, Dr. deVeber and his wife and family decided to move to Lethbridge in 1890. The deVebers returned to Fort Macleod in May 1890, to a thank you party from an appreciative community. Dr. deVeber was presented with a gift of surgical instruments, as a reflection of the esteem in which the community held the deVebers.[26]

1890-1905 The Lethbridge (NWT) years

In Lethbridge, Dr. deVeber joined Drs. A.M. Lafferty and F.H. Mewburn, in time to see the Galt Hospital opened in 1891.[27] His practice included assisting Dr. Mewburn at surgery and giving anesthetics.

Dr. deVeber continued his civic contributions in his new community, by joining the Lethbridge Board of Trade and by being appointed to its Executive Committee. In 1895 he acquired the Lethbridge Drug Company and moved into the back section of the drugstore.[28] In April 1898 he was appointed the Medical Officer of Health (MOH) for Lethbridge.[29] In his first presentation to the Chairman of the Health and Relief Committee, Dr. deVeber reported one case of measles and one of diphtheria. The latter he quarantined for six weeks. In July of 1898 he was appointed a Justice of the Peace. In August 1898 he was appointed the Lethbridge Municipal Sanitary Inspector under the Contagious Disease Ordinance. That appointment paid no stipend.[30]

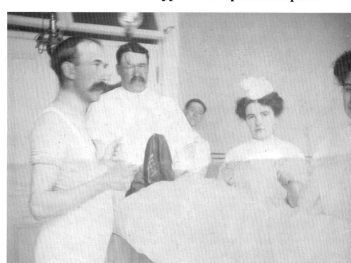

Above - Operating room of the Galt Hospital in Lethbridge, 1891. Dr. Frank H. Mewburn at left, Dr. deVeber, a young Walter S. Galbraith peaks around the corner, unknown nurse and nurse Gladys Hamilton. The patient was not identified. Galt Archives GP19861093000

In 1898 the sitting MLA, Mr. C.A. Magrath, resigned as the member of the NWT Legislative Assembly for Lethbridge. Dr. deVeber was nominated to succeed him. He was elected by acclamation. During his first term, he participated in the revision of the 1902 NWT Public Ordinance Act on sanitation.[31]

In his 1901 MOH report, Dr. deVeber reported he had supervised the care of fifteen cases of smallpox, eight of scarlet fever, one of typhoid and one of chickenpox. Three of the scarlet fever cases proved fatal. He urged the Town Council of Lethbridge to erect an isolation hospital. The one placed at his disposal was makeshift at best.[32] At least he got one, likely by persuading Mayor (Dr.) Mewburn of the need for it.

In 1902 Dr. deVeber ran again for the NWT Legislative Assembly. He won the election against "Billy" (later Justice) Ives.[33] During the 1902-1905 session he was appointed the Government whip. As well he advised Laurier on how to handle the separate school question that had been raised by the Mormons.[34] When the province of Alberta was formed in 1905, Dr. deVeber ran for a third time, this time as a Liberal. He was elected to the first Alberta Legislature and was appointed by Premier Rutherford as Minister without Portfolio in the first Alberta Cabinet.[35]

Dr. L.G. deVeber represented the area on the Legislative Assembly of the North West Territories from 1898 to 1905, before Alberta became a Province in 1905.   Glenbow Archives NA-433-23

1905-1923   The Lethbridge (Alberta) years

Shortly before the first Alberta Legislative Assembly in May 1906, Prime Minister Laura appointed Dr. deVeber as the first Senator from the Province of Alberta. He was joined by veterinarian Dr. Percy Talbot. They were the third and fourth NWT/Alberta Senators to be appointed and followed William Hardisty 1888-1889 and James Lougheed 1889-1925.[36] Dr. deVeber's first speech in the Senate was described as "breezy, and to the point, going straight to the matter of hand, along the line of public improvements". This apparently meant it was about highways and bridges. The local newspaper opined that "his successor will find a high mark set for services rendered".[37]

In the Senate he was appointed to the Public Health and Food Inspection Committee and industriously represented the west.[38] After Prime Minister Laurier came to Edmonton to cut the ribbon and officially dedicate the new Alberta Legislature in 1910, he toured the province. Dr. deVeber and his wife hosted the Lauriers in Lethbridge.

The deVebers made annual trips to Ottawa for many years. Unfortunately his political success wrecked havoc with his once flourishing practice. Dr. deVeber approached Dr. Peter Campbell of Cardston in 1905 to entice him to move to Lethbridge. Campbell did his own research. At Dr. deVeber's suggestion he met Dr. F.H. Mewburn, the now well known and widely respected southern Alberta surgeon. "Mewburn was most kind, praised deVeber as a man, said there was room for another white man anywhere, and advised me to come". This I think must be a classical example of two men each trying to stand so straight that they leaned over backwards.[39]

Campbell never changed his mind. He remained of the opinion that deVeber was "a square shooter, endowed with an abundance of human kindness, always charming, courteous, and hard-working. His word was as good as his bond."[40]

Dr. deVeber continued to practice with Dr. Peter Campbell for ten years. The clinic they started continues today as the Campbell Clinic. Dr. deVeber was also President of the Southern Alberta (Lethbridge) Medical Society and remained active in the Board of Trade and the International Order of Foresters and Elks.

In his remarks to a post 1913 graduating class of Galt Hospital nurses, Dr. deVeber welcomed them into their profession and congratulated them on their chosen ideal, of alleviating the sufferings of humanity. He emphasized that womanhood was the best preparation for the ideal nurse.[41]

Dr. deVeber retired from medical practice and as the Lethbridge MOH in 1915. deVeber was called back into practice during the Spanish flu epidemic of 1918/19. He supervised the thirty-five bed emergency hospital, that handled the hospitalizations for the 2579 flu cases. Tragically it included 129 deaths.[42] The deVebers maintained their home in Lethbridge until 1923 where they were well known for their rose garden.

1923-1925   The Ottawa years

In 1923 the deVebers permanently moved to Alymer, Quebec near Ottawa. Shortly after his death on July 9, 1925 at age seventy-six, Dr. (Senator) deVeber had the distinction of becoming one of Alberta's first six (of seven) Senators, after whom a mountain in the Canadian Rockies was named.[43] He joined Sir James Lougheed in that acknowledgement. Mount deVeber, a peak 8494 feet high (2 589 m), was the mountain which Dominion Surveyor A.O. Wheeler climbed in 1923, to take his last circumferential photographs from the camera platform on its summit. The triangulations from the top of Mount deVeber were the most northerly survey points recorded during Wheeler's ten year survey of the Alberta/BC border.[44] Mount deVeber is located twenty miles (32 km) west of Grand Cache. It was challenged for the first time by members of the deVeber family, on Aug. 9-20, 2002. A plaque was deposited at the base of the last buttress to commemorate the event.[45]

The deVebers had two children. Marion Francis was born in late 1885 or early 1886. She was raised in England. She married a ship builder and remained there until late in her life. Her brother Leverett Sandys was born in 1894, but was discouraged from entering medicine by his father. Instead he joined the Bank of Montreal. Rachel deVeber lived nineteen years longer than her husband and died on January 17, 1944 in Ottawa. She lived long enough to see two deVeber grandchildren enter medicine. Barrie became a Pediatric Hematologist and George a Nephrologist. The deVeber medical dynasty has continued into the next generation. Two of Dr. deVeber's great-grandchildren chose medicine as well. Gabrielle deVeber became a pediatric neurologist and Hiliary deVeber a pediatrician. Some day the deVebers may rival the seven consecutive generations of physicians in the Mewburn family.

Galt Archives GP19760229039

Dr. Frank Hamilton Mewburn, OBE, MD, FACS
1858 - 1929

*"His was a personality that a student encounters rarely.
None...could fail to be influenced by the joyous way
that he went into battle for his patient
he was...completely patient - centered...
He was first, last and always the doctor."* [1]

Introduction

Frank Hamilton Mewburn arrived in Winnipeg in March 1882, just in time to play a significant part in the most eventful era in Surgery in Western Canada. No one who came and stayed did more to lead the advance than this diminutive McGill trained, self-taught surgeon.

The arrival of the CPR changed the Canadian West forever. It reached Winnipeg in 1881, Regina in 1882, Calgary in 1883, and Craigallachie in 1885. So did the formation of the Manitoba Medical College in 1883, the first and only western medical college for the next thirty-one years. The 1872 Winnipeg General Hospital (WGH) was moved and enlarged to 72 beds in 1884. The Northwest Rebellion brought 5,800 soldiers and 43 physicians to the North West Terriories in 1885; and the first scheduled transcontinental trains in 1886.

With the promise of peace following the Northwest Rebellion, came the first wave of immigration to the "free lands". Following in lock-step were the pioneering medical practitioners, druggists and pharmacies, hospitals and operating rooms (OR's). With these pioneers came improved sanitation measures and expectations that eastern metropolitan standards of medical care would be imported into the west.

The 1880's also saw the dawn of intra-abdominal surgery in the western medical world.[2] Dr. Mewburn arrived at the beginning of major abdominal surgery and evolved with it, as it became a specialty within medicine. He was a pioneer in the Mackid tradition.[3]

Driven by impetuosity, surgical audacity and a streak of rugged independence, Dr. Mewburn headed west from Winnipeg to the end of the "Turkey Trail" railway line, at Lethbridge in 1886.[4] Early Lethbridge was then known as Coal Banks. There he met his intellectual and medical soul mate, Dr. G.A. Kennedy, who after eight years with the NWMP entered full-time private practice in Fort Macleod in 1887. The knowledge and experience of these two medical pioneers, coupled with their operative skills and astute diagnostic decision-making, led to a remarkable string of surgical and medical accomplishments. In retrospect the citizenry of Lethbridge and Fort Macleod must have marveled at their good fortune to have them come and stay in their communities.

In true frontier tradition, both Drs. Mewburn and Kennedy answered many calls from their fledgling communities, to contribute beyond their daily medical practices and on-call schedules. Mewburn responded thrice as mayor and never declined the requests of the Boards of the Public School, of the hospital, and the business institutions of Lethbridge, for more of his time and attention.[5]

As Mewburn's surgical reputation grew, his referral radius widened. Financially secure and with a 1913 Charter Fellowship in the American College of Surgeons (FACS), he moved to Calgary and polarized his practice to surgery on a full-time basis. On the eve of WWI, Dr. Mewburn accepted the position as Senior Surgeon at the Calgary General Hospital (CGH).

In 1914 the call of patriotism and the challenges of wartime surgery beckoned. Mewburn had already had a taste of it during the Northwest Rebellion. He had not participated in the Boer War, probably because the Medical Corps was run by the British Army and the expected one-year tenure of the Lord Strathcona Horse, was too short to entice a physician to join the medical militia. And besides, he was the Mayor of Lethbridge.

Deemed over age by the WWI Minister of the Militia, Sir Sam Hughes, Mewburn was refused enlistment. Not dissuaded, he went to England at his own expense and joined the Canadian Army Medical Corps (CAMC). At Taplow, he was rapidly promoted to the Head of Surgery - Canadian General Hospital #5.

Two years after his 1919 demobilization, the new University of Alberta (UofA) Dean of Medicine, A.C. Rankin approached Mewburn over Dr. Edgar A. Allin and Dr. John S. McEachern to become the first full-time head of Surgery at the UofA. With that appointment came the challenge of extending the medical curriculum by two years and creating a full six-year Medical School program with degree granting status. It was one of the conditions of the 1920 University of Alberta Rockefeller Grant. So was the creation of a clinical training program in medicine and surgery. By December 1923, all conditions were met, or were in the process of being met, releasing the $500,000 grant to the University of Alberta and eventually to the Faculty of Medicine.

While his string of prairie surgical firsts is unrivaled, it was his love of teaching and the respect he received from his students, that left Dr. Mewburn's greatest imprint on medicine in Alberta. Unfortunately his career was cut short in 1929 while he was still in harness. It brought to a halt Mewburn's desire to record the highlights, impressionable experiences, events, friendships and colleagues, that he regretted had not been undertaken sooner.[6]

1858-1875 As a Youth

Frank Hamilton Mewburn was born on March 5, 1858, the youngest of seven children, in Drummondville, Ontario, now part of Niagara Falls. He grew up to be a skinny, pigeon breasted, five foot six inch, 140 pound, cherubic, physically frail student. To increasing his presence Mewburn grew a "walrus" type moustache. His full head of hair complemented his great personal charm.

When Mewburn decided to enter medical school circa 1875, he became the fourth of an eventual seven-generation physician dynasty that exceeded two hundred consecutive years of medical service. The first, his great-grandfather Dr. Francis Mewburn, commenced his medical studies by apprenticing under Thomas Hornby in 1765. His grandfather Dr. John Mewburn obtained his Membership in Royal College of Surgeons (MRCS) and was honourably mentioned by Sir Astley Cooper. He chose to come to Canada in 1832. His father Dr. Francis Clarke Mewburn apprenticed with his grandfather in Weston, near Toronto, before moving to Niagara Falls. Francis C. Mewburn was awarded an honourary Doctorate in Medicine by the University of Buffalo in New York.[7]

1875-1882 Medical School

No sooner had Dr. Frank Mewburn commenced his medical studies at McGill, than another wonderful event happened. In 1875 four trained nurses from St. Thomas Hospital in London, England arrived at the Montreal General Hospital. Until then nursing was done by "handy" women.[8] The importance of nurses to medicine, and the importance of nurses in the eyes of Dr. Mewburn, would resurface in 1923. That year Dr. Mewburn and two other physicians restarted the three-year RN and five year nursing degree program at UofA.[9]

While still a student at McGill he saw his first ovariotomy or removal of the ovaries. It must have excited him and provided an early stimulus for his career in surgery. Mewburn became an early disciple of the Lister Carbolic Fog technique, no doubt introduced to it at McGill by Dr. Thomas Roddick who had visited Lord Lister in 1875.[10] The value of Lister antisepsis was likely reaffirmed by his experiences treating the injured that came to the Winnipeg General Hospital (WGH) during the CPR railway construction period[11] and three years later by the same Dr. Thomas Roddick, who was appointed the Deputy Surgeon General and senior Field Surgeon during the 1885 NW Rebellion.[12]

1882-1885 Winnipeg General Hospital (WGH) and the NW Rebellion

After graduating in 1881, Dr. Mewburn interned for a year at the Montreal General Hospital, with Drs. John A. Macdonald, James Bell and Andrew Henderson.[13] The next year he moved to the booming town of Winnipeg. In March 1882 he was appointed the WGH's House-Surgeon, a role expanded in 1884 to one as the Chief Resident Officer, with general charge of the fourteen or more staff and the seventy-two beds. He could not practice, only consult. While Dr. Mewburn could admit emergencies, he spent most of his time attending to the patients of the staff physicians.[14] Although the Manitoba Medical College (MMC) started in Winnipeg in November 1883, Dr. Mewburn was not one of the thirteen charter members, founders or instructors.

In 1885 Dr. Mewburn's responsibilities were extended to provide care for the patients sent to the new WGH military wing, during and after the 47 day NW Rebellion.[15] Dr. Thomas Roddick closed the Saskatoon base hospital July 7, 1885, and transferred the last seventeen NW Rebellion casualties one thousand miles by barge, down the Saskatchewan River, across Lakes Winnipeg and Winnipegosis to the WGH. Dr. James Kerr, the Dean of the MMC was responsible for the admission, management and the treatment of the transferred casualties. Dr. Mewburn was responsible for their ward care.[16]

Dean Kerr was a surgeon at the WGH. He performed three operations on the 81 soldiers hospitalized: 1) an excision of a large hydrocele of the neck that was anatomically in contact with the carotid sheath, 2) an incision and drainage of an empyema, and 3) an incision of a knee joint to extract a bullet.[17] Likely Dr. Mewburn assisted Kerr as the Chief Resident Officer. In August 1885 when Dr. Roddick returned to

Winnipeg from the east, ten patients remained in the WGH.[18] Some stayed until the next spring before being transferred back to Ontario.

1886-1913 The Lethbridge Years

Despite these experiences and opportunities, Dr. Mewburn became increasingly frustrated by the limited amount of surgery he was getting at the WGH.[19] Although the hospital had seventy-two beds, Mewburn noted that up to 1886 when he left, there had been only two or three abdominal operations[29] that he could have seen.[20] On the invitation of Elliott T. Galt, the Lethbridge coal mine owner he assessed the surgical-administrative opportunity in the burgeoning coal town. He left Winnipeg at -40C and arrived on December 2, 1885 in Lethbridge during a Chinook. On his arrival, there was no snow and everyone was in shirtsleeves. Enthused, Mewburn soon returned to Lethbridge to live permanently, when his WGH contract expired in January 1886.

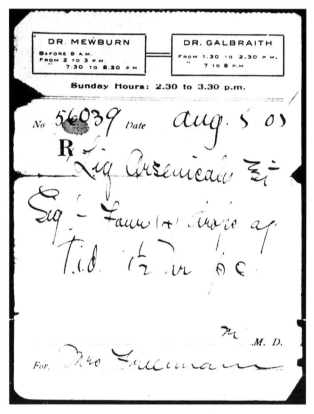

An early prescription written by Dr. Mewburn August 5th 1905.
From the Calgary Association Clinic Historical Bulletin, page 52

Dr. Mewburn was appointed the medical manager of the newly constructed three bed Police and Mine Hospital, as well as the NWMP Acting Assistant Surgeon. There he joined NWMP Hospital Sergeant, E.A. Braithwaite.[21] After he registered under the NWT Medical Ordinance, Mewburn became the first official (NWT) doctor in Lethbridge.[22] On August 15, 1886 Dr. Mewburn received a visit from his former teacher, Dr. (later Sir) William Osler and his brother, CPR shareholder Edmund B. Osler.[23] The next year 1887, Mewburn accepted the hand of Prince Edward Island-born Louise Augusta Nelson as his wife. Louise had come to Lethbridge as a governess for the children of the Assistant Mine Manager.[24]

In 1891, with the financial help of mine owners, father and son Sir Alexander and Elliott Galt, the hospital was increased from three to twelve beds. It was renamed the Galt Hospital and included an operating room (OR) in the attic. The OR was likely the fourth one in Alberta.[25] After operating on a tubal pregnancy, Mewburn wrote of his experience in his first article in medical literature. It was published in February 1893, in the Montreal Medical Journal.[26] The patient had initially refused surgery. That delayed the operation eleven days. After receiving approval, a laparotomy was immediately performed. Massive amounts of blood were found in the lower abdomen. The patient rallied briefly then passed away later that day.

As the only physician in Lethbridge, Mewburn was offered and accepted several early medical contracts. His NWMP medical contract was extended from 1886 to 1911. In 1911 Drs. E.A. Braithwaite and Mewburn were appointed the only two honourary NWMP surgeons in Alberta. Mewburn's honourary NWMP appointment continued until 1929, making him the second-longest RCMP surgeon in the Force at forty-three consecutive years. It was five years shorter than Dr. E.A. Braithwaite's appointment.[27] Dr. Mewburn also held the railway medical contract from Medicine Hat to Great Falls, and participated in the CPR medical construction contract during the building of the Crowsnest Pass rail line in 1899.

Surgical Experience in Lethbridge

Dr. Mewburn had no contract to provide medical care to the Blood Indian Reserve. That didn't stop members arriving at his doorstep. In 1887 he diagnosed one patient as having an enlarged goiter. An interesting ceremony followed. Mewburn solemnly harangued the patient and the Indians accompanying him. "I shall have to make a big cut. If you all do as I tell you after the big cut is made this man may get well, but I cannot tell for sure until after I have made the big cut; and then if he does not get well, and if he should die you must not blame me. What do you say - shall I make the big cut?" "Ugh, Ugh, Ugh" came the reply from the sick man and his friends. The operation was a success.[28] His reputation amongst the natives was established. Dr. Mewburn became known amongst the Indians of the NWT as "The Great Big Medicine Man."[29] No doubt it reflected more on his competence, than as a metaphor on his size.[30]

Francis Coulson described Mewburn's first recorded intra-abdominal operation in Lethbridge. It was to drain an abdominal abscess in 1887. Dr. Mewburn operated in a local saloon using a pool table as his OR table.[31] A barber gave the Chloroform anesthesia, a reversal of the historical origins of surgery. The most likely source of the abscess would have been a perforated appendix. The patient recovered. Authors F.S. Coulson and Drs. Hugh Arnold and Peter Campbell reported this operation as the first appendectomy west of Winnipeg. Henri Chatenay and Dr. A.G. Stanley agreed but recorded the operation as being performed in 1889.[32] Dr. Walter Stewart Galbraith disagreed with all of them and described Mewburn's first planned appendectomy as being performed in 1893.[33] J.D. Higinbotham, Dr. H.E.

Rawlinson and Alex Johnston agree with Galbraith.[34] In all probability Galbraith is correct as his testimony indicated.

In 1893 the future Dr. W.S. Galbraith was working as an assistant to pharmacist, J.D. Higinbotham of Lethbridge. Interested in learning about medicine, Galbraith asked to watch Dr. Mewburn, during what he (Galbraith) called Mewburn's "first" appendectomy. In an Appreciation to Dr. Mewburn after his death, Dr. Galbraith said it was his privilege, "then only looking on, to watch his development from surgery of amputations and abscesses to his first appendectomy in 1893. That patient had traveled two hundred miles to have it done and it had evidently ruptured sometime before, and everything was in a terrible mess as they nearly all were in those days, before early interference was permitted." It is doubtful if the appendix was removed, but the patient got well and with increasing ease, cases were offered for his skill; hernias in plenty, an ectopic gestation which he reported, until December 10, 1903 came the climax as he (Mewburn) then thought, in a Caesarian section. His progress from that point was continuous.[35]

Mewburn appeared to confirm the 1893 date, as his first appendectomy. He told his students, "I have seen several patients die with "perityphlitis" (the original name for appendicitis) and I had noticed articles appearing in the journals suggesting that the condition was essentially a purulent inflammation of the appendix and early resort to surgery was advocated. I determined that the next case (which likely is the one Dr. Galbraith described) that came along I would operate on without delay".[36]

Mewburn's most audacious surgery was performed on November 15, 1890 in Fort Macleod. The patient had an osteomyelitis and an un-united leg fracture. Drs. Mewburn and G.A. Kennedy did the surgery and were assisted by Staff Sergeant Braithwaite. Bone chips from a dog's leg were inserted into the NWMP carpenter's un-united fracture site, following "Olliers Procedure", as it had recently been described in the French and American medical literature. Post-operatively the graft did not take, so Mewburn and Kennedy removed the chips in early 1891 in Lethbridge.[37] The patient lived for over another forty years, albeit with one leg two inches shorter than his other good leg.[38]

Another early operation Mewburn performed was on a strangulated hernia. Mewburn said to the elderly gentleman, "I think you are going to die, but operating is the only thing I can do". The operating table was a meat block under a tree. The local butcher, and a well-known Lethbridge citizen Mr. C.B. Bowman, were pressed into action as the assistant and the anesthetist. One would assist until gastric heaving gained the upper hand, whereupon the other pallid assistant would relieve him. The patient survived.[39]

In 1888 Alberta's early orthopedic surgeon Dr. Reginald Deane, FRCS, met Mewburn as a youth, when he was growing up in Lethbridge. He was told that Mewburn was "a wizard with the knife". The first operation Deane was allowed to watch was on a ninety-year-old gentleman with senile gangrene of the right hand.[40] Mewburn amputated the arm through the middle of the humerus. Deane's duty was to hold up the arm. The operation was performed in the unfinished attic of the old Galt hospital. The patient survived. Deane recorded Mewburn operating on another case of intestinal obstruction, in a room over a livery stable. The liveryman poured the anesthetic and a roustabout worked as a helper. Deane's third recollection was in 1898, after he had entered practice in Lethbridge. Dr. Mewburn asked him to see a patient with a kidney stone. Dr. Deane recommended chemical dissolution of the stone, using a new German drug "Urotropine". Mewburn said quizzically, "You think so?" A couple of days later the cutting took place and a stone the size of a pigeon's egg was removed from the kidney.

Usually, abdominal surgery was done on a last ditch basis, which made it even more difficult.[41] The same was likely true in the Saskatchewan case where the first laparotomy was performed by Dr. M.M. Seymour in Fort Qu'Appelle.[42] If it was performed in a public hospital, it would have been after 1899, when, the first public hospital was built in Saskatchewan.[43]

Dr. Peter Campbell wrote that Mewburn was a slow surgeon and he had to give an anesthetic for five and a half hours, while Mewburn excised the patient's bilateral varicose veins. That patient survived too. Another example was a thyroidectomy, which took over two hours.[44]

To keep medically current Dr. Mewburn made yearly pilgrimages to visit the great surgeons of his day, especially to Baltimore, where his lifelong friend Dr. William Osler was the Professor of Medicine. Every night Mewburn would read the surgical literature for two hours. As patient confidence in his judgment increased, his reputation spread and his surgical practice enlarged.[45] To keep diagnostically current, Dr. Mewburn bought the Galt hospital their first x-ray machine at his own expense.[46]

1889-1913 Medical and Community Affairs

Dr. Mewburn attended the 1889 Canadian Medical Association (CMA) annual meeting in Banff. He was a charter member of the NWT Medical Association, which was formed after that meeting.[47] Seventeen years later in 1906, he was appointed to the first Board of the College of Physicians and Surgeons of Alberta and remained on it from 1906-1913, becoming the College President in 1912-1913.[48] He was also appointed to the first provincial Board of Health 1907-1910 and made significant contributions to it and the CMA.[49]

Mewburn was well-known in Lethbridge. He made daily rounds on horseback until 1910, even though he owned a car and had a chauffeur to drive it.[50] His energy level was inexhaustible. But he always found time for his community.[51] He sat on the Lethbridge School Board, the Board of Trade, and the Town Council and was Mayor in 1899, 1900, and 1905. In real estate he admitted he was lucky, when he bought nine lots adjacent to his home, including three ostensibly to avoid a Chinese Laundry being built next door. He paid less than $1,000 for them. Thirteen years later he sold the lots for $90,000 cash.[52] Before leaving Lethbridge in 1913, he wrote off $50,000 in unpaid services, because the patients "didn't have a bean and so he charged it to the Lord". That same year Dr. Mewburn received his FACS, the first year they were granted, and moved to Calgary (population 43,700). There he was appointed the Chief Surgeon and limited his practice to surgery at the Calgary General Hospital.[53] The move united Dr. F.H. Mewburn with his older brother Lloyd T. Mewburn, who had moved to Calgary in 1903.[54]

Below: Dr. Mewburn often made his medical rounds on horseback
Galt Archives GP19754296000

1914-1921 Mewburn and WWI

In 1914 the Minister of the Militia, Sam Hughes refused Dr. Mewburn's application to join the Canadian Army Medical Corps (CAMC), because he was too old at age 55. Mewburn wired back, "Reference your wire - go to hell! I'm going anyway."[55] He cabled Dr. William Osler, telephoned his cousin Brigadier General S.G. Mewburn, and "pulled wires" through Prime Minister Robert Borden and Colonel Sam Steele, to be taken on as a Major.

Dr. Mewburn paid his own way to England. His wife accompanied him. He was "taken on strength and posted to Depot C. CAMC", Shorncliffe, England on July 1, 1915. The posting was confirmed three weeks before the Mewburns left Canada on July 21, 1915.[56] Dr. Mewburn was transferred to the #5 Canadian General (Duchess of Connaught) Red Cross Hospital at Taplow on the Astor Estate, Clivedon, on September 9, 1915. He remained there except for two temporary transfers back to the CAMC Medical Depot from Feb. 22 - May 10, 1915 and March 15 - April 17, 1917.

Dr. Frank Hamilton Mewburn in military attire after serving in World War I.
University of Alberta Archives (Jamieson Collection) 81-104-4-41

Dr. Mewburn was promoted to Lieutenant Colonel on August 14, 1916 and was made Second in Command of the Taplow Hospital on April 17, 1917. His second secondment to the CMAC Depot, in March/April 1917, overlapped with Dr. E.G. Mason's first month at the Depot. The two were both there during the Battle of Vimy Ridge and the capture of the two highest points by Lt. Col. Mason's 50th Battalion on April 9-12, 1917.[57] Lt. Col. F.H. Mewburn was made an Officer of the Order of the British Empire (OBE) on June 7, 1918.[58]

The chief medical consultant at Taplow was Sir William Osler. The two gentlemen spent many happy weekends together in London, England. Osler procured a book for him mentioning the Mewburn Family, which he autographed "to the brilliant son of a more brilliant father".[59] It became one of Mewburn's prized possessions. In May 1919 Lt. Col. Mewburn was demobilized and returned to Calgary, where he resumed his practice and continued to limit it to surgery.

1921-1929 University of Alberta's
First Professor of Surgery

In 1921 Dr. Mewburn accepted an offer from the 1920 appointed University of Alberta (UofA) Dean of Medicine, Dr. A.C. Rankin to become the first full-time Professor of Surgery. In Dr. R.B. Deane's testimonial to Mewburn at his 1921 Calgary farewell banquet, Deane highlighted Mewburn's "insatiable appetite for work, attention to detail whether large or small, and treatment of the rich and poor equally."[60]

Funding for Mewburn's UofA Faculty of Medicine position came from interest on the $500,000 1920 Rockefeller Foundation conditional grant to the UofA. Two of the conditions were to appoint the first clinical teachers in surgery and medicine and to complete a full six-year medical degree-granting program. Drs. Mewburn and Egerton Pope were appointed full-time faculty positions in surgery and medicine respectively, at the funding level of $5,000/year.[61]

After moving to Edmonton, Dr. Mewburn resumed his surgical practice from an office in the McLeod building. With the assistance of Dr. H.C. Jamieson, Dr. Mewburn started the popular medical/surgical bedside rounds, in the Osler tradition. In December 1922, Mewburn was elected the first Chairman of the University of Alberta Hospital (UAH) Medical Advisory Board, shortly after the University reassumed responsibility for the old Strathcona Hospital, from the Soldiers Civilian Re-establishment Commission, and renamed it the University of Alberta Hospital (UAH).[62]

The University Hospital where Dr. Mewburn supervised the surgical department.
From: Dr. R. Lampard collection

In 1923, the three-year RN and five-year nursing degree programs were restarted at the UAH. Dr. Mewburn, along with UofA President H.M Tory and Dean A.C. Rankin, were identified as the three persons most instrumental in the development of those two programs.[63] The nursing students adored Mewburn. He would come for morning rounds with a retinue of students singing in high falsetto "...every little movement has a meaning all its own. He wore a rose in his buttonhole...and always a fresh lab coat, shiny white and crisp.... He had a chauffeur, Lawrence, who always dressed in a grey uniform...he'd been the Colonel's batman overseas."[64] There were many colorful stories told by "The Colonel's" friends and students about Mewburn's care for his patients.[65] It was considered beyond reproach. He would move his patient to a private room if they were disturbing others and would pay for it and any special nurses, himself.

Below: The Department of Veterans Affairs Col. Mewburn Hospital part of the University of Alberta Hospital in Edmonton, Alberta.
From: Dr. R. Lampard collection

In 1925, the "J.J. Ower Reporting Club", which was the first medical literature review "club" started for the senior medical students, was renamed the Mewburn Club. Dr. Ower the future Dean of Medicine, continued as its secretary from 1920-1959.

In 1927, Dr. Mewburn was elected the second Vice-President of the American College of Surgeons,[66] one year after Dr. J.S. McEachern of Calgary held the position.

Dr. Mewburn's medical bibliography of four articles is short.[67] He was a good writer and speaker, but neither were a priority. After he gave a UofA presentation, on Lord Lister and his antiseptic technique,[68] he was asked to give the speech on CFRN radio Edmonton. When he discovered that Dr. E.A. Braithwaite had been a student of Lord Lister, the responsibility for the presentation was quickly transferred.

In harness to the last, Dr. Mewburn operated all one day with his son Hank, only to miss his chauffeur and walk home in a winter storm. He developed pneumonia and succumbed four days later on January 29, 1929,[69] leaving behind two sons, one of whom (Dr. F.H.H. Mewburn) was the first Professor and Head of Orthopedics at the UAH. His other son Arthur entered the oil business. The Mewburns also had a daughter Helene.[70] A grandson, Dr. Robert Mewburn, became a Psychiatrist and practiced in Vancouver. Robert Mewburn passed away in 1977, ending the Mewburn medical dynasty at seven consecutive generations, or 212 continuous years, including 145 years in Canada.[71]

Below: A plaque commemorating Dr. Frank Hamilton Mewburn, professor of surgery at the University of Alberta Medical School.
UofA Archives.

1929 In the End

In his testimonial, Dean Rankin described Dr. F.H. Mewburn as an energetic, self-sacrificing, unselfish, man of integrity; a wise and respected counselor and a sympathetic associate and friend. Dr. W.S. Galbraith, his partner in Lethbridge for six years, didn't credit Mewburn with scholastic brilliance, but did reflect on his keenness to follow known techniques; his surgical daring, and ever present persistence to learn, whether it was from colleagues, books, journals or yearly pilgrimages to the clinics of the great surgeons. Mewburn's epitaph, he said, was to give his best; to succeed with what you have. "He was straight forward to friend and foe alike and his friendship highly prized".[72]

At Dr. Frank Hamilton Mewburn's request, his coffin was wrapped in a Union Jack, carried on a gun carriage flanked by a Mounted Police Guard of Honour, followed by a saddled horse with Mewburn's boots reversed and a military band.[73] In his Will, Mewburn gifted his medical library, including his many journals to the UofA. Along with the Edmonton Academy of Medicine's Library, it formed the core of the UofA Medical Library.[74]

The UofA awarded him an Honourary Doctorate in 1922 one year after his alma mater McGill did. A plaque commemorating Dr. Mewburn as the first full-time Professor of Surgery was placed by the UofA Board of Governors in the entrance hall of the old Medical Building. It acknowledged his "more that forty years with the practice and teaching of medicine in western Canada. A life securely built into the Foundation of this Province".[75]

A monument erected on June 1937 at the Galt Hospital in Lethbridge commemorating Lt. Col. Mewburn. Galt Archives GP19891049121

The Dr. F. H Mewburn Chapter of the Imperial Order Daughters of the Empire (I.O.D.E.) was formed in 1930. A cairn in front of the Galt Hospital in Lethbridge was unveiled in 1937. It was christened with wild flowers by Blood Chief, Chief Shot Both Sides.[76] The Mewburn Pavilion for returning Veterans was built in Edmonton on the UAH site at the end of WWII in 1945, and named after him. The Mewburn Gold Medal in Surgery continues to commemorate his pioneering contributions to surgery in Alberta.

Dr. Frank Hamilton Mewburn OBE, MD, CM, LLD, FACS, 1856 - 1929.
University of Alberta Archives (Jamieson collection) 81-104-4-42

Dr. Mewburn may have been short in stature,
but he cast a long shadow over the practice
of Medicine and Surgery in the NWT and Alberta.

Dr. George Henry Malcolmson, MD
1868-1944

*"He has journeyed widely in search of knowledge
bringing to our specialty (Radiology)
that enviable prestige, in the sunshine of which we
bask".[1]*

University of Alberta Archives (Jamieson collection) 81-104-77

Introduction

Dr. George Henry Malcolmson was Alberta's pioneer radiologist. He brought the first x-ray unit to Frank, Alberta in 1906. In 1915 he became the first full time radiologist in Edmonton. In 1919 he and Dr. Edgar Allin bought the first radium in Western Canada. Dr. Malcolmson was the first Director of the Alberta Cancer Service starting in January 1941. That clinic provided the first free cancer treatment services in Canada.

1868-1897 From Youth to MD

George Henry Malcolmson was born on April 7, 1868 in Hamilton, Ontario. He entered medical school with John S. McEachern at the University of Toronto (UofT) and graduated in 1896 at the age of 27. 1896 was the year the first x-ray machine arrived at the UofT. X-rays had been identified one year before in Germany by W.K. Roentgen in 1895.

After a year of internship at the Hamilton General Hospital, Malcolmson made a life-long decision to spend two months out of every two years investigating medical practices in more advanced centres in North America. Through those continuing educational trips he would meet and befriend Drs. Osler, Kelly, Halsted, the Mayo Brothers and many other notable physicians and medical teachers.[2]

1897-1911 Lethbridge and the Crowsnest Pass

In 1897 Dr. Malcolmson packed his medical bag and headed west to start a practice in Lethbridge. There he joined Dr. F.H. Mewburn as a general practitioner and anesthetist for one year. He registered as a physician in the NWT on September 5, 1898.[3] At the end of his one-year with Dr. Mewburn, he signed a contract with the Canadian Pacific Railway to serve as their Medical Health Officer, during the construction of the Crowsnest Pass Railway. That moved him to the more windy Pincher Creek country, where he established a general practice and discharged his CPR medical contract duties.[4]

In 1901 Dr. Malcolmson moved his practice another thirty miles westward to the coal town of Frank. By scrimping his pennies, he was able to open one of Alberta's first rural hospitals in 1902. It was an annex to his house. His wife was one of the three nurses. Another nurse was pioneer Calgary General Hospital Nurse, Mary Moodie, who joined Malcolmson in 1902 for a year and a half.[5]

The 1903 Frank Slide

On April 29, 1903 at 4:10 A.M. the Malcolmson house shuddered and shook as Turtle Mountain fractured and eighty million tons of rock avalanched down its north side, narrowly missing Malcolmson's home, the adjacent annex and most of the town of Frank. Ten percent of the town was destroyed.[6] There were seven houses in the path of the slide.[7] Canada's most deadly landslide lasted about one hundred seconds.[8]

Tragically about seventy Frank residents died as a direct result of the huge slide. Twelve bodies were recovered.[9] Four of the ten were seriously injured. Together with the walking wounded, they were sent to Dr. Malcolmson's "hospital", which luckily was still intact. Malcolmson's worst case was from the windblast, which drove a board into the patient's abdomen. Feathers from the patient's bedspread were blown into the wound at the same time. Malcolmson removed each imbedded feather, one at a time.[10] One patient had a splinter that penetrated the liver. Another had a broken hip. One suffered shock from internal injuries and stone splinters which were embedded like a pincushion.[11] All of Malcolmson's hospitalized patients survived.[12]

After the initial rockslide, sporadic smaller rockslides continued for the next forty-eight hour period. Fortunately there were no more major avalanches. Seventeen miners were trapped underground. Surface miners worked round the clock at the slide site to reach the miners trapped underground. On April 29, thirteen hours after the slide, the seventeen trapped miners dug their own way to freedom, through twenty-nine feet of coal and limestone.[15] One rescued miner had a fractured leg. The rest walked to Dr. Malcolmson's temporary infirmary. Earlier that day Drs. O.C. Edwards and George A. Kennedy arrived by train from Fort Macleod, with a team of nurses and a contingent of NWMP officers. For the physicians and their volunteers it was a short stay. The four serious casualties in the hospital were beginning to recover. The triage team returned home almost immediately.[16]

Wanting an "on the spot" story, the Winnipeg Free Press sent David A. Stewart, the future Manitoba tuberculosis leader and medical historian, to cover the unfolding Frank slide story. The year before, Stewart had spent the summer of 1902 as a theology student minister at Frank. Dr. Malcolmson had convinced him to switch his studies from theology to medicine, which he did. Stewart probably stayed at the Malcolmson home, for the weeks he was in Frank, helping Dr. Malcolmson during the day, while writing Free Press articles in the evening.[13] Stewart also conducted one of the first assessments of the Turtle Mountain fracture, by climbing the mountain on May 1, 1903.[14]

A view likely witnessed by reporter David Stewart on May 1st, 1903 from atop Turtle Mountain peering over the edge of the recent Frank Slide.
Galt Archives GP19760216020

Because of the threat of flooding, as well as another slide, Premier F.W. Haultain and CPR chief engineer A. McHenry, decided to evacuate the town on May 2, 1903. The injured, who lay in beds in the annex, and Dr. Malcolmson's living room, were loaded aboard special railcars and transported one and a half miles to the NWMP barracks. The NWMP helped by moving out under canvas, and turning their barracks into the temporary Frank emergency hospital.[17]

A Geological Survey assessment of Turtle Mountain was commissioned on April 30, 1903. Two experienced Dominion Surveyors were sent to the site: R.G. McConnell and R.W. Brock.[18] In their June 12, 1903 report, the surveyors concluded that the mountain was very unstable. That didn't close the mine. Instead new entry shafts were dug away from the slide site. Then in 1905 there were two serious fires and more seepage from the nearby lake. Coal mining operations continued at Frank until 1911, when new warnings were issued by the Geological Survey. That closed the mine. Most of the remaining Frank businesses relocated further west to Blairmore in the Crowsnest Pass. Dr. Malcolmson moved as well.

1906   The first x-ray machine in Alberta

During an educational trip to Boston in 1906, Dr. Malcolmson's interest in x-rays was kindled. He became so excited by their potential, that he bought an x-ray machine and brought it back to his hospital in Frank that same year.[19] It was the first x-ray unit in a rural hospital, if not the first in Alberta, arriving the same year as the units arrived in Edmonton and in Saskatoon.[20] X-rays were not new to Western Canada. A decade earlier the first glass prints had been made in Winnipeg.

Above: A view of the hospital in Frank, Alberta, likely the site of the first X-ray equipment in Alberta.   Glenbow Archives NA-5074-4
Below: Nurse Moodie in the Frank Hospital tending to a patient.
Glenbow Archives NA-5074-5

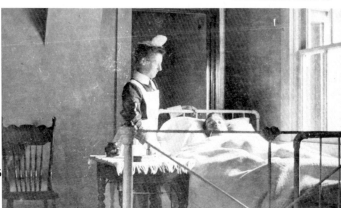

There is no indication how often either Drs. Malcolmson in Frank or E.A. Braithwaite in Edmonton used their early machines. Nor is there any publication of a spectacular "first case", as documented by Dr. M.S. Inglis in Winnipeg in 1896 who had used an x-ray to settle a legal suit.[21] If it was a "Victor" model similar to Dr. E.A. Braithwaite's unit brought to Edmonton in 1906, they took twenty minutes to wind up.[22]

1911-1915 General Practice Years in Edmonton

In 1911 Dr. Malcolmson took another medical education break, traveling to Europe to study x-ray practices. The Frank mine closed, so Dr. Malcolmson moved to Edmonton and joined the staff of the new Royal Alexandra Hospital (RAH).[23] Dr. Malcolmson was already well known in Alberta's medical circles. He had been the Vice President of the Alberta Medical Association in 1907/08, and would be the President of the Alberta College of Physicians and Surgeons in 1914/15.[24] In 1911 the College of Physicians and Surgeons asked the UofA to examine candidates wishing to register to practice medicine in Alberta. In 1912 Dr. Mewburn was appointed to the first Board of Examiners in Medicine, by the Senate of the University of Alberta (UofA).[25]

The value of x-rays continued to impress Dr. Malcolmson. His interest grew. It was fostered by the x-ray diagnosis of renal tuberculosis in one of his kidneys, at the Mayo Clinic in 1914. The diagnosis had been missed by the physicians at the Johns Hopkins Hospital one week before. Dr. Will Mayo removed Malcolmson's kidney.[26] In 1911 the College of Physicians and Surgeons had asked the UofA to examine candidates wishing to register for practice medicine in Alberta.[2] He remained tuberculosis free for the rest of his life. The same year, 1914, Malcolmson was elected President of the renamed Edmonton Academy of Medicine and joined the Allin Clinic in Edmonton.[27]

1915-1941 The Radiology years in Edmonton

In 1915 Dr. Malcolmson became the first full-time Alberta Radiologist, as well as the first primarily hospital based radiologist, at the Royal Alexandra Hospital. That was three years before Dr. W. Herbert McGuffin, who had bought an x-ray unit for his private office practice in 1911, became a full-time radiologist in Calgary, in 1918.[28]

In 1919 Dr. Malcolmson, along with Dr. Edgar Allin purchased the first supply of radium for the treatment of cancer in Western Canada.[29] In 1924 Malcolmson left the Allin Clinic and became a full-time hospital based radiologist. About the same time, he was appointed a Consultant in Radiology at the University of Alberta Hospital (UAH), under Radiology Department Head Dr. Richard Proctor. When the RAH was renovated in 1928, Dr. Andrew F. Anderson set aside a substantial amount of main-floor space for Radiology, to the chagrin of the medical staff. In return, Dr. Malcolmson installed the first high (KVH) generator in Alberta.[30]

Dr. Malcolmson continued to base his work at the RAH and practice full-time radiology through the 1920's and 1930's. He was particularly helpful to the orthopedic surgeons, until felled by another personal illness. He developed cancer of the bladder in 1936. Palliative surgery was performed. Recurrences shortened his life, but not before his son Pat joined him in the practice of Radiology in 1938.

1941-1944 The Alberta Cancer Clinic

On January 1st, 1941 Dr. Malcolmson's son, Dr. Patrick H. Malcolmson took over the Malcolmson radiology practice. That was the date the Alberta government introduced free diagnostic Cancer Clinic services in Canada. Dr. Malcolmson Sr. accepted the appointment as the first Head of the Alberta Cancer Clinic and the physician in charge of the UAH Cancer Clinic in Edmonton effective that day.[31]

Dr. George H. Malcolmson

Longtime friends of Dr. George Malcolmson, like J.O. Baker, recognized his inquisitive mind, as far back as his years in Frank, Alberta. He was one of the first physicians to use a microscope for making a diagnosis and grow or culture bacterial specimens for his patients. At one time his Crowsnest Hospital was a centre of such medical activity that he had four assistants working for him.[32]

Dr. G.H. Malcolmson enjoyed relaxing on the golf course. Another interest was playing the violin. He had taken violin lessons as a youngster and maintained his competence until x-ray damage to his fingers made it impossible. He was Provincial Commissioner for the Boy Scouts of Canada.[34] For his patients he had the delightful habit of wearing a rose in his coat lapel or under his lead apron when he was working in the x-ray room, bringing a fresh aroma to those he treated. He was a well-known Christmas Santa Claus to the children in the Cancer Clinic and always carried extra candies in his pockets for special occasions.

In recognition of his thirty-three years of work in the field of Radiology, and for his many contributions to the Canadian Association of Radiology, the Association presented Dr. Malcolmson a gold-headed cane in 1939. Dr. W.H. McGuffin made the presentation and acknowledged Dr. Malcolmson as the first full-time Radiologist in Alberta and one of the first in Canada.[35]

The Malcolmson Family

Dr. George Henry Malcolmson met his future wife while on a house-call to Blairmore from Lethbridge in 1898. The two nursed his future sister-in-law, through a prolonged illness. The Malcolmsons had five children: three daughters and two sons. Daughter Norah joined Dr. Malcolmson as an early x-ray technician. Another daughter died of diphtheria at age two, despite an emergency tracheotomy performed by her father. Striking miners refused to dig the grave so Dr. Malcolmson dug it himself.[33] One son, Patrick became a second generation Radiologist in Alberta.

Dr. George Henry Malcolmson died on February 28, 1944 at the age of 76.[36]

Footnotes:

Dr. Richard Barrington Nevitt

1 Ells, S.C. — From Northland Trails, as quoted by Dr. J.B. Ritchie in Early Surgeons of the North West Mounted Police Part V, Doctor Richard Barrington Nevitt, Calgary Associate Clinic Historical Bulletin (CACHB) 22(4): 249, February 1958.

2 Ritchie, J.B. — NWMP surgeons (in Saskatchewan), CACHB 22(3): 210-218, November 1957. Surgeon #3 was Dr. R. Miller, who was stationed at North Battleford/Prince Albert starting October 25, 1875. Surgeon #4 was Dr. G.A. Kennedy of Fort Macleod. He started in October 1878.

3 Price, E.B. — "Doc" Lauder, Alberta History 37(4): 28-31, Autumn 1989. John D. Lauder was recruited with the "third" NWMP detachment in Ottawa in 1876 as a Hospital Sergeant. He had three years medical training in Dublin. 800 applied for the less than 100 recruits that were hired. Lauder was at the signing of Treaty #7 in 1877 and described it in detail. He was stationed at Fort Calgary for most of his four years in the Force. He also attended the death of Crowfoot at Gleichen in 1890. Drs. E.A. Braithwaite and L.G. deVeber were also contracted as Hospital Sergeants by the NWMP.

4 Nevitt, R.B. — A Winter at Fort Macleod, edited by Hugh Dempsey, 134 pages, Glenbow, 1974.

5 Kittson, J.G. — Report of Surgeon John Kittson, Swan River, December 19, 1875, pages 19-30 in A Chronicle of the Canadian West: North West Mounted Police Report for 1875. Reprinted by the Historical Society of Alberta, 1975.

6 Cameron, I.H. — Richard Barrington Nevitt: an Appreciation, CMAJ 19: 282-283, 1928.

7 Jamieson, H.C. — Early Medicine in Alberta, pages opp 16, 17-23, AMA, 1947. Nevitt graduated from UofT with an MB in 1874. Eight years later in 1882, he would earn his full MD.

8 Ritchie, J.B. — Early Surgeons of the North West Mounted Police: Part V. Doctor Richard Barrington Nevitt, Assistant Surgeon: 1874-1878, CACHB 22(4): 249-265, February 1958.

9 Higgitt, W.L. — The Act respecting the Administration of Justice, and for the establishment of a Police Force in the North West Territories. Assented to 23 May 1873. Reprinted in Opening Up the West. Reports of the Commissioners of the North-West Mounted Police 1874-1881, Coles Canadiana 1973.

10 French, G.A. — Report of the Commissioner dated January 18, 1875 to the Minister of Justice from Winnipeg, page 6. The whole report is reprinted as Appendix A, in Opening Up the West, Coles Canadiana, 1973.

11 Nevitt, R.B. — A Winter at Fort Macleod, page 8.

12 Ritchie, J.B. — Early Surgeons of the North West Mounted Police: Part V, page 252.

13 Ritchie, J.B. — Early Surgeons of the North West Mounted Police: Part V, pages 252-254.

14 French, G.A. — Report of the Commissioner, dated January 18, 1875, page 19.

15 French, G.A. — Report of the Commissioner, dated January 18, 1875, pages 8, 19.

16 French, G.A. — Report of the Commissioner, dated January 18, 1875, page 9.

17 Turner, J.P. — The North-West Mounted Police 1873-1893, Vol. I: 123, Kings Printer, 1950.

18 Turner, J.P. — The North-West Mounted Police 1873-1893, page 130.

19 Kittson, J.G. — Report of Surgeon John Kittson, pages 19-26.

20 Ritchie, J.B. — Early Surgeons of the North West Mounted Police: Part V, page 156. It was the largest and longest sick parade of any day on the March.

21 Kittson, J.G. — Report of Surgeon John Kittson, page 21.

22 Kittson, J.G. — Report of Surgeon John Kittson, December 19, 1875, pages 22-23. Kittson held a sick parade at an Indian camp nearby. The Chief presented 3 of 9 males and 5 of the 7 women in the camp. Kittson diagnosed one as nearly blind, 1 with sciatica, 1 paralysis agitans, 2 dysentery, 3 phthisis (chronic lung disease). They all gave up his prescriptions, after a few days.

23 Turner, J.P. — The North West Mounted Police: 1873-1893, pages 172-173.

24 Kittson, J.G. — Report of Surgeon John Kittson, December 19, 1875, pages 23-24. It originated when the Troop camped at an old Indian Camping ground. They were out of Mercurial ointment they had brought to treat for such problems.

25 French, G.A. — Report of the Commissioner, page 24.

26 (Nevitt, R.B.) — Site plan for Fort Macleod, opposite page 76. Reprinted in Opening Up the Canadian West, Coles, 1973.

27 Hartwick, E., Jamieson, E., & Tregillus, E. — At Your Service, Part One, Medical Services, the Act, the Service and the Spirit, page 300, Volume 5, Century Calgary, 1975. Also reprinted in H.C. Jamieson's Early Medicine in Alberta opposite page 32.

28 Nevitt, R.B. — A Winter at Fort Macleod. Letters edited by H.A. Dempsey, 134 pages. Glenbow, 1974. The first one was dated October 11, 1874 and was published in the Savannah newspaper (5, p11). The rest were sent to "Dear Lizzie" with the last dated June 14, 1875. There were 145 in total. An equivalent number appear to have been written by Elizabeth "Lizzy" Beaty back to Dr. Nevitt. As well there were newspapers and letters from Nevitt's sister Saide, who returned to Georgia in 1875. Unless otherwise quoted, all comments are from Nevitt's letters to Lizzy.

29 Jamieson, H.C. — Early Medicine in Alberta, page 22, AMA 1947. For more information on John D. Lauder, see E.B. Price's "Doc" Lauder, in Alberta History 37(4): 28-31, Autumn 1989. She interviewed John Lauder circa 1929. Also see Hilda Neatby's The Medical profession in the North-West Territories, Saskatchewan History 2(2): 3-4, 1949, and R. Lampard's profile of Dr. Henry George reference #27, for comments on this early colourful politician.

30 Jamieson, H.C. — Early Medicine in Alberta, page 22.

31 Kittson, J.G. — Report of Surgeon Kittson, Swan River, December 19, 1875, pages 24, 29.

32 Reprinted in Opening Up the West, pages 33-35, Coles Canadiana, 1973.

33 Kennedy, G.A. — Report of Surgeon Kennedy, November 30, 1879 to Col Macleod. Reprinted in Opening Up the West, pages 33-35, Coles Canadiana, 1973.

34 Beahen, W., Horrall, S. — Red Coats on the Prairies, pages 187-192, 207. Centax Books, 1998.

35 Kittson, J.G. — Report of Surgeon John Kittson, December 19, 1875, pages 19, 26. Dr. Kittson refers to the climate as "so much vaunted by the doctors out East for its bracing effects on the lungs...a question of much importance and open to many sided views. ...I offer no theories as to the effects of high or low altitudes and latitudes, but merely report the few cases that have come under my notice." He then described 3 cases of (clinical) tuberculosis, that had all recovered.

36 Turner, P. — The North West Mounted Police I: 169, Kings Printer, 1950.

37 Jukes, A. — Endemic Fever in the North West Territories, in the Supplement to the Northern Lancet, pages 1-16, January 1890.] Dr. Jukes, the Senior NWMP surgeon from 1882-1892, recommended 10 grains of Quinine, to be repeated in one hour if the temperature had not increased. This procedure was to be repeated until a remission of 24 hours has been established. He based it on the treatment used by the "medical officers of the Army of the Potomac", during the American Civil War.

38 Oko, A.J. — The Frontier Art of R.B. Nevitt, page 50.

39 Ritchie, R.B. — Early Surgeons of the North West Mounted Police: Part V, page 262.

40 Ritchie, R.B. — Early Surgeons of the North West Mounted Police: Part V, pages 250-251.

41 Ritchie, R.B. — Early Surgeons of the North West Mounted Police: Part V, page 251 (check).

42 Oko, A.J. — The Frontier Art of R.B. Nevitt. The Canadian Collector 11(1): 46-50, Jan/Feb. 1976. A selection of 16 of Nevitt's watercolours were included in a brief article on Richard B. Nevitt: Mounted Police Artist in Alberta History 29(4): 18-25, Autumn 1981.

44 Chalmers, J.W. — The Mounties' First Artist in Great Stories from the Canadian Frontier, pages 61-65, Antonson Publishing, 1979.

43 Oko, A.J. — The Frontier Act of R.B. Nevitt, page 50.

45 Ritchie, R.B. — Early Surgeons of the North West Mounted Police Part V, page 262.

46 Ritchie, R.B. — NorthWest Mounted Police V, pages 250-251.

Dr. George Kennedy

1 Ells, S.C. — Northland Trails (n.d.) as quoted by J.B. Ritchie in George Alexander (sic) Kennedy, MD, 1858-1913, Canadian Journal of Surgery 1: 297, July 1958.

2 Stanley, G.D. — George Allan Kennedy (1878-1913) Calgary Associate Clinic Historical Bulletin (CACHB) 5(2): 7-10, August 1940. Dr. Andrew Everett Porter (1855-1940) arrived in the summer of 1878 at Prince Albert, Saskatchewan shortly before Kennedy arrived in Fort Macleod, CACHB 6(2): 5-11, August 1941. He moved several times first to Coleman, Alberta in 1893, then to Nova Scotia from 1893-1910; before returning to Edmonton from 1910-1940, CACHB 6(3): 10, November 1941. The second physician to stay in Alberta for the lifetime of his practice was Dr. H.C. Wilson (Edmonton, 1882-1909) and the third was Dr. L.G. deVeber (Fort Macleod, 1882-1891 and Lethbridge 1891-1915).

The first NWMP physicians to practice full time in the NWT were Drs. Kittson, Nevitt, Miller and Kennedy. The first physician to practice part time in the NWT was Dr. George Verey (Edmonton, 1872-81). Other early short stay physicians included "Doc" J. Lauder (Calgary NWMP, 1878-1881); Drs. L.J. Munro (Edmonton, 1882-86); O.C. Edwards (Regina, 1882-89, Fort Macleod, 1901-15); A. Henderson (Calgary, 1883-87). There were HBC physician/fur traders in Rupertsland as early as 1668.

3 Kennedy, G.A. — See the NWMP annual reports as reprinted by Coles Canadiana in 1973. The four volume covering the period 1874 to 1889 and containing the following NWMP Surgeon reports:

I. Opening Up the West 1874-1881; Official reports of the North-West Mounted Police. Report of Surgeon J.G. Kittson, 1879, Fort Walsh, pages 27-33, January 30, 1880. Report of Surgeon G.A. Kennedy, 1879, Fort Macleod, pages 33-35, November 30, 1879. Report of Surgeon G.A. Kennedy, 1880, Fort Walsh, pages 44-49, December 23, 1880.

II. Settlers and Rebels: Official reports of the North-West Mounted Police, 1882-1885. Report of Surgeon G.A. Kennedy, Fort Walsh, 1881, pages 28-32, January 1882. Report of Surgeon G.A. Kennedy, 1881, for Forts Macleod and Wood Mountain, pages 33-34, February 1, 1882. Report of Surgeon A. Jukes, 1882, Fort Walsh, pages 24-30, November 29, 1882. Report of Surgeon G.A. Kennedy, 1882, Fort Macleod, pages 32-34, December 4, 1882. No reports in 1883. Report of Surgeon A. Jukes, 1884, Regina, pages 25-31, December 22, 1884. Report of Surgeon G.A. Kennedy, 1884, Fort Macleod, pages 34-36, December 5, 1884. Report of Surgeon G.A. Kennedy, 1885, pages 91-92, November 30, 1885. Report of Surgeon A. Jukes, 1885, Regina, pages 83-89, December 5, 1885.

III. Law and Order: Official reports of the North-West Mounted Police, 1886-1887. Report of Surgeon G.A. Kennedy, 1886, Fort Macleod, pages 90-92, December 1, 1886. Report of Surgeon A. Jukes, 1886, Regina, pages 79-89, December 16, 1886. Report of Surgeon A. Jukes, 1887, Regina, pages 98-103, December 30, 1887.

IV. The NewWest: Official reports of the North-West Mounted Police, 1888-1889. Report of Surgeon A. Jukes, 1888, Regina, pages 141-144, December 26, 1888. Report of Surgeon G.A. Kennedy, 1888, Fort Macleod, pages 167-169, December 29, 1888. Report of Surgeon A. Jukes, 1889, Regina, pages 126-131, December 20, 1889.

4 Neatby, H. — The Medical Profession in the North West Territories. Saskatchewan History 2(2): 1-16, May 1949.

5 Kerr, R.B. — The History of the Medical Council of Canada, pages 18-26, MCC 1979. The first page of the Canadian Medical Register and a photo of members of the first Medical Council November 7-9, 1912 are opposite page 66. Dr. Kennedy together with the Board of the MCC, became the first registrants. Alberta representatives on the first MCC in alphabetical order were Drs. Brett (registration #5), Kennedy (#14) and John Park (#25).

6 Bliss, M. — William Osler. A Life in Medicine, pages 44, 57, 68-69, 73, 79, UTP, 1998. After leaving his home in 1866 at age 17, Osler returned to Dundas in 1868 and 1869 to assist Dr. Holford Walker. After graduating from McGill in 1872, Osler did locums in Hamilton and Dundas in 1872 and 1874. He wrote frequent letters home to his parents as well. Osler's first mentor was the naturalist Rev. W.A. Johnson of Toronto. Osler dedicated his 1892 Principles and Practices of Medicine to Rev. Johnson, and Drs. Bovell and Howard. Rev. Johnson's son Andrew Jukes Johnson took medicine at Toronto and McGill at the same time as Osler. Dr. Augustus Jukes was Rev. Johnson's brother-in-law (see R.B. Deane's Augustus Jukes, CACHB 2(4): 1-5, February 1938).

7 Betke, C. — Kennedy, George Allan. Dictionary of Canadian Biography 1911-1920, Volume 14: 556-558, 1998.

8 Ritchie, R.B. — Early Surgeons of the North West Mounted Police, Part III(2) Dr. George Alexander (sic) Kennedy, CACHB 22(2): 210-212. The roster of 33 early NWMP surgeons lists only surgeons who served in the North West Territories and later in the province of Saskatchewan. It omits early NWT physicians who served (full time, part time or on contract) in the NWT and later Alberta: Drs. deVeber (1882), Henderson (1883), Braithwaite (1884), Mewburn (1886), Lafferty (1886-9), Rouleau (1885-1910) and many more. The overall total for both provinces is unknown but probably approaches 100 full time and part time physicians.

Where possible the NWMP entered into shared Indian Affairs or part-time contracts. After 1881, the Kennedy contract was cost shared with Indian Affairs. Dr. Kittson's contract had been split in 1879. He provided care to the Sitting Bull's Sioux at Wood Mountain. In Dr. Kennedy's case the nearby reservations were members of the Blackfoot Confederacy, the Bloods and Peigans. No full time physician was retained to provide medical care on the Indian Reservations until 1883.

9 Ritchie, R.B. — Early Surgeons of the North West Mounted Police, Part III(1) Dr. George Alexander (sic) Kennedy, CACHB 22(2): 171-173, August 1957. Also see R.B. Ritchie's Early Surgeons of the North West Mounted Police, RCMP Quarterly 23(3): 233-236, January 1958.

Mark Twain (Samuel Clemens) was on a part-time contract with the US Government to give lectures, on the responsibilities of new settlers, at Fort Benton, Helena and Silver City, Montana. Kennedy wrote his first letter home describing his Missouri trip and his visits with Twain. The letter(s) were in Dr. J.B. Ritchie's possession or were shown to him for reference purposes, when he wrote his CACHB articles in 1957 and 1958. Kennedy repeated one Twain story on the subject of education. "When I was a boy of fourteen my father was so ignorant that I could have hardly stood to have him around. But when I got to be twenty-one, I was astonished at how much he had learned in seven years". Kennedy said this story struck him as funny, but he was glad and happy his parents had taught him to adhere to the straight and narrow path in life.

10 Ritchie, R.B. — Early Surgeons RCMP Quarterly 23(3): 233-234. From reading Kennedy's letter(s) to his parents, Ritchie concluded that "his (Kennedy's) own purpose in life...could be envisioned" by one of the verses in Gray's Elegy Written in a Country Churchyard that Twain quoted:

"Far from the madding crowds ignoble strife,
Their sober wishes never learned to stray;
Along the cool sequestered vale of life
They kept the noiseless tenor of their way".

Unfortunately the Kennedy letter(s) have not been found despite a search of National and RCMP and Fort Macleod Museum archives. The family archival material was given to the Fort Macleod Museum, as confirmed by Dr. Kennedy's granddaughter Barbara Stevens of Victoria, BC, during an interview with the author on March 19, 1995.

11 LaDow, B. — The Medicine Line: Life and Death on a North American Borderland, pages 29-32, Routledge, 2002.

12 Stuart, R. — Lion of the Frontier, pages 67-69, 1979. Constable Holtorf, whose life Steele had saved the previous winter, nursed him, riding miles for a daily pail of cold water. The "last" night Holtorf crept in to Steele's room but Steele awoke and asked why. When told, an amused Steele guffawed and ordered him out. The fever broke the next morning. It was many days before Steele could walk without a cane. Slowly he recovered but he never recovered his temporary loss of memory. The illness is discussed in S.B Steele's "Forty Years in Canada", pages 145-146, McGraw-Hill, Ryerson, 1972 edition.

13 Kittson, J.G., & Kennedy, G.A. — Annual Report of Surgeon Kittson written at Fort McLeod, NWT, January 30, 1880 and Annual Report of Surgeon Kennedy written at Fort Macleod, NWT, November 30, 1879. Reprinted in Opening Up the West 1874-1881, Coles Canadiana pages 27-35, 1973 and in R.B. Ritchie's Early Surgeons III(2) CACHB 22(2): 201-204, November 1957. Kittson reported the fever first (re)appeared at Fort Walsh in 1876 (one case). In 1877 there were several mild cases admitted to his Fort Walsh hospital. He reported 11 cases in 1878 (3 typhomalaria type); 17 in 1879 (all typhomalaria type). Kennedy thought the severe or lethal form occurred when typhoid was superimposed on malaria. No deaths occurred in the NWMP ranks in 1879 but two did amongst the white population (Mr. Clark and William Walsh). Many Metis and Indian children died.

14 Kennedy, G.A. — Annual Report of Surgeon Kennedy written at Fort Walsh, NWT, December 23, 1880. Reprinted in Opening Up the West 1874-1881, pages 44-49, Coles Canadiana, 1973 and Early Surgeons III(2) Doctor George Alexander (sic) Kennedy, 204-210, CACHB 22(3), November 1957.

15 Beahen, W., & Horrall, S. — Red Coats on the Prairies - the North West Mounted Police 1873-1900, pages 186-189, Centrax 1998. Also see Early Surgeons III(2), Doctor George Alexander (sic) Kennedy, CACHB 22(3): 204, November 1957.

16 Decker, J.F. — Surgeons' Stories, Beaver 78(3): 24-27, June-July, 1998.

17 Price, E.B. — "Doc" Lauder, Alberta History 37(4): 28-31.

18 Kennedy, G.A. — Annual Report of Surgeon Kennedy, Fort Walsh, NWT, December 23, 1880, pages 44-45. Kennedy records no cases of "mountain fever" at Fort Walsh in 1880, although there were five cases of "intermittent fever". Kennedy gave three reasons for the paucity of cases that year: 1) great attention to sanitation, 2) experience of former years, and 3) the nature of the season (dry spring).

"Mountain fever" as Kennedy was now calling it, reoccurred in 1881 with 13 cases at Fort Walsh (see the annual report of Surgeon Kennedy written at Fort Walsh, January 1882, pages 28-31). The next year there were 38 cases by October 15, 1882 as reported in the Annual Report of Surgeon Kennedy written at Fort Macleod December, 1882 in the Official reports for 1882.

19 Girard, F.X. — Macleod Gazettes of June 28, 1883 and August 29, 1884. For more information on Dr. Girard's remuneration and competence see Maureen Lux's Medicine That Walks, pages 143-146, 154, UTP, 2001.

20 Duncan, J. — Red Serge Wives, page 20, 1974.

21 Kennedy, G.A. — Annual Report of Assistant Surgeon Kennedy written at Fort Macleod, December 4, 1884, pages 34-35, 59. The hospital consisted of two wards holding about 10 cots/beds. There was a 10' x 20' surgery/dispensary and three other small rooms. Other contemporary hospitals on the prairies included Winnipeg (1872, 20 beds, increased to 72-80 beds in 1883); Missoula Montana (1873/4, 19 beds). The largest NWMP hospital was built in Regina (1887, 25 beds). For the Montana description see The Sisters Hospital in Montana, the Magazine of Western History 53(1): 35, Spring 2003. For the Fort Macleod floor plan see the Report of the Commissioner of the NWMP, (1883, A.G. Irvine), page 59, in Settlers and Rebels 1882-1885, Coles Canadiana 1973.

22 Higinbotham, J.D. — Notes from "When the West was Young", pages 65-79, Ryerson 1933. Reprinted by Bruce Haig, Lethbridge Herald, 1978. Also see the F.H. Mewburn profile.

23 Tolton, Gordon E. — The Rocky Mountain Rangers, page 64. Occasional paper #28, Lethbridge Historical Society, 1994. The book includes a discussion of Dr. deVeber's involvement in the NW Rebellion of 1885. Also referenced in G.D. Stanley's Archives Column, George Allan Kennedy, Alberta Medical Bulletin (AMB) 16(3): 64-65, August 1951.

24 Godsal, F.W. — Old Times. Alberta Historical Review 12(4): 20, Autumn 1964.

25 Higinbotham, J.D. — J.D. Higinbotham Fonds, Glenbow M517, Box 4, File 24 Diary 1885. "Dr. Kennedy's house was completed by January 25 and a place of frequent social activity".

26 Higinbotham, J.D. — When the West was Young, pages 66-67. See K. Penley's the History of Pharmacy in Alberta, page 43, 1993, for more information on Higinbotham.

27 den Otter, A.A. — Urban Pioneers of Lethbridge, Alberta History 25: 19, 1977. For more information see the J.D. Higinbotham's Fonds, Glenbow M517, Box 4, file 24 Diary 1885 and Higinbotham's letter to Dr. P.M. Campbell of February 18, 1930 in the H.C. Jamieson Papers, UofA archives, 81-104, Box 21/1/1-14.

28 Ritchie, R.B. — George Alexander (sic) Kennedy, MD, 1858-1913, Canadian Journal of Surgery 1: 279-286, July 1958. Almost every year Kennedy visited clinics in eastern Canada and the USA. Dr. Peter Campbell notes in his article on Frank Hamilton Mewburn, that Mewburn read Surgery two hours a night, CACHB 15(4): 61-69, February 1951.

29 Hogan, D.B. — Osler Goes West. Annals RCPSC 33(5): 316-319, August 2000. Osler then the Chief of Medicine at Philadelphia, traveled west for four weeks during August 1886. The first transcontinental CPR train had crossed Canada in June 1886. In July 1886 Sir John A. Macdonald and his wife came west. For a 1886 photo of the eastern returning Macdonald party (sans Sir John A.) see C.A. Magrath's The Galts and Early Life in Lethbridge, pages 38-39, circa 1929, deposited in the Lethbridge Galt Museum.

Osler was accompanied his older brother Edmund, a large CPR shareholder; Messrs. Begg, Burns and Bains from Edinburgh; and Peter White the Southern Alberta MP. They left Toronto August 4. With stopovers and side trips, the party reached Lethbridge on August 15, as noted in the Lethbridge News of August 18. They reached Fort Macleod August 16 and Calgary August 18. Dr. J.D. Lafferty hosted them in Calgary. Whether Osler saw Brett in Banff is unknown. The party traveled to Vancouver and were back in Winnipeg by August 24 and Ontario sometime after August 26.

Osler was President of the CMA in 1884-85 but missed the annual meeting on August 18-19, 1886 because of the western trip. If Osler met Kennedy it is likely they discussed the "typhomalaria" problem at the NWMP Forts, which is possibly why Kennedy re-proposed to standardize the definition and reporting of it by Fort, so a "treatise" could be authored, as noted in his December 1886 NWMP report.

In Kennedy's 1890 NWTMA Presidential Address, he makes a comment on the "rarity of pneumonia and other affections of the lungs. Speaking of the Indians...(an) extremely interesting question...in answer to the question asked by the worthy President of the Canadian Medical Association, that I have made careful enquiries of the veterinary surgeons and stockmen of Alberta, and that as yet, no case of Tuberculosis has been discovered on the Alberta ranges". Was the reference to CMA President Osler (1884/85, Internist), Ross (1889/90, Surgeon) or Roddick (1890/91, Surgeon)? A copy of his Presidential speech in Medicine Hat is located in the H.C. Jamieson Papers at the University of Alberta.

In all probability Drs. Jukes, Osler and Kennedy all knew each other from their days in St. Catharines, Toronto, and Dundas, Ontario.

30 Kennedy, G.A. — In his November 1885 report Dr. Kennedy records the first (8 in total) cases of mild "malarial" fever at Fort Macleod in the Official Reports for 1885, pages 29, 30 and another 38 cases at Fort Macleod in 1886 including one death. A marked increase occurred after "D" Division arrived in Fort Macleod in September 1886 following the Battleford outbreak of typhoid fever, as it is now known. He recommended a collective investigation by all NWMP surgeons. Kennedy was disappointed when Jukes refused, in his report on December 16, 1886, pages 79-89. Mewburn recounted Kennedy's impressions in his Life and Work of Dr. George Allan Kennedy, CMAJ 21: pages 327-328, 1929.

31 Kennedy, G.A. — Presidential address, Dr. G.A. Kennedy Med. Hat 2nd annual N.W.T.M.A. 1890. 8 typed pages. In the H.C. Jamieson Papers, UofA archives #81-104, Box 1/1/1-26. Kennedy spent 3 of the 8 pages in his NWTMA speech on the topic of typhoid fever. He called it an addressable, preventable, treatable but a widespread prairie problem.

The first Winnipeg General Hospital was built in 1872 to treat cases of typhoid fever. During the NW Rebellion strict adherence was paid to hospital location, hygiene and removal of privies. There were four cases of typhoid fever amongst the 5000 troops. One died of typhoid - Lieutenant Colonel Williams as recorded in John Pennefather's Thirteen Years on the Prairies, page 54, 1892. The Battleford outbreak of typhoid fever caused 5 NWMP deaths in 1886. From 1886-1900 there were twenty-three NWMP deaths from typhoid (of 96 deaths in total) as reported in Beahen and Horrall's Redcoats on the Prairies, pages 191-192, Centax 1998. There were several more cases including two deaths during the 1874 NWMP March and one more in October 1874 in Fort Macleod.

32 Johnston, A., et al — Lethbridge Its Medical Doctors, Dentists, Drug Stores. Occasional Paper #24, pages 6, 32, Lethbridge Historical Society, 1991.

33 Kennedy, G.A. — Case of Penetrating Bullet Wound. Canadian Practitioner, pages 377-379, December 1888. C.C.M is most likely C.C. M'Caul or C.C. McCaul. He is the young lawyer referred to in J.D. Higinbotham's When the West was Young, page 88 and in Kennedy's article on the Climate in Southern Alberta of 1889, pages 2-3. The

Macleod Gazette of August 29, 1884 prints an advertisement by McCaul. Mewburn discusses the McCaul case in the Life and Work of George A. Kennedy without naming him, indicating most such patients die, CMAJ 21: 328-329, 1929.

34 Ridge, A.D. — C.C. McCaul Pioneer lawyer. Alberta History 21(1): 21-25, Winter 1971. He died August 10, 1928 at age 71. Ridge summarizes the fascinating life of the restless, talented McCaul.

35 Kennedy, G.A. — The Climate of Southern Alberta and its Relation to Health and Disease. Montreal Medical Journal, pages 1-11, October 1889. Kennedy was already using the name Alberta, as introduced by the Postal Service.

The subject or the origin of Chinook winds in the northwest was presented in 1) the Transactions of the Royal Society of Canada (#22), 1886 and by 2) C.C. McCaul in the August 1888 issue of the American Meteorological Review, as referenced in Dr. G.A. Kennedy's article on The Climate of Southern Alberta, pages 2-3.

The quest or "competition" for tuberculosis patients continued with J.H. O'Donnell the Superintendent of the WGH promoting Winnipeg because of its dry, sunny and barometrically stable temperature, in the Northern Lancet, pages 39-41, 1891.

36 Lampard, R. — First CMA meetings in Alberta/NWT (August 11-12, 1889) in the Alberta Doctors Digest 29(4): 4-9, July/August, 2004.

37 Hogan, D. — Calgary, Climate and Tuberculosis. Annals of the RCPSC 35: 430-434, October 2002. Calgary's Mayor promoted Calgary as a TB destination circa 1895, giving geographic similarity to Denver as his reasons. The CPR were willing to subsidize the travel west for TB patients. Little concern was shown over their infectious nature on the railway cars. William Gage of Ontario proposed Kamloops for a Sanatorium. When that occurred, the Calgary bid was killed. No application was successful until William Gage lobbied for a National Sanatorium Association, which was established by an Act of Parliament in 1896. He then contributed to the construction of the first sanatorium at Muskoka Lakes, Gravenhurst, Ontario. It was opened in 1897.

Kennedy still strongly supported his climate thesis in his NWT annual Hospital Inspection reports 1898-1901 in the NWT (see the report for each year).

38 MacDermot, H.E. — The 22nd annual meeting at Banff in 1889. CMAJ 54: 496-498, 1946. 89 attended. 82 paid. The audience exceeded 150 (including wives, non-members). 83 were in the official Woodruff photograph (see Jamieson's Early Medicine in Alberta opp, page 48). The special CPR train left Montreal August 6 and included Upper and Lower Canada, Maritime physicians plus 9 US physicians. There were 17 physicians from the NWT and one from Winnipeg (Dr. H.H. Chown). For more details see R. Lampard's The CMA Convention of 1889. Alberta Doctors Digest 29(4): 4-9, July/Aug, 2004.

39 Jukes, A. — The Endemic Fever of the Northwest Territories. Supplement to the Northern Lancet, pages 1-16, January 1890.

40 Kennedy, G.A. — The Climate of Southern Alberta and its Relation to Health and Disease. Montreal Medical Journal, pages 1-11, October 1889.

41 Deane, R.B. — Augustus Jukes, A Pioneer Surgeon. CACHB 29: 1-4, February 1938.

42 Jamieson, H.C. — A Short Sketch of Medical Progress in Alberta, CMAJ 20: 188-190, 1929. Jamieson, without naming his source, wrote "It is a matter of record that the reader of the paper was regarded by the members as an enthusiast who had lost his sense of judgment". Dr. F.H. Mewburn who was there recounted, "The first paper produced a profound sensation in this meeting...well reasoned coming from a comparatively young man living in the country, was unexpected and took them by storm", CMAJ 21: 327, 1929.

43 Mewburn, F.H. — The Life and Work of Dr. George A. Kennedy, page 329. "Some time afterward the (NWMP) headquarters provided the Macleod post with an up-to-date pocket case of efficient surgical instruments". Editorial RCMP Quarterly 12(3): 177, January 1947.

44 Johnston, A., et al — Lethbridge Its Medical Doctors, Dentists, Drug Stores, page 9, 1991.

45 Stanley, G.D. — George Allan Kennedy, CACHB 5(2): 7-10, August 1940.

46 Kennedy, G.A. — Presidential Address, Dr. G.A. Kennedy, Medicine Hat 2nd annual meeting, NWTMA, page 4. (H.C. Jamieson)

47 Jamieson, H.C. — Marion E. Moody, The First Nurse to Graduate in Alberta. CACHB 4(4): 7-10, February 1940.

48 Thomas, L.H. — Early Territorial Hospitals. Saskatchewan History 2(2): 16-20, Spring 1949. Kennedy was the only NWT hospital inspector from 1897-1905 (CMAJ 21: 327). His inspections included general hospitals as well TB treatment centres, as noted in M.E. Robinson's history of nursing in Saskatchewan entitled: The First Fifty Years, pages 17-19, 1967. For further information see the NWT Department of Agriculture annual public health hospital inspection reports prepared by Dr. Kennedy from 1898-1907.

49 Kennedy, G.A. — Letter to Honourable Clifford Sifton, Minister of the Interior, January 14, 1901. 4 pages. Copy in the NWT archives, Regina, reference #80470-80473. In it Kennedy quotes the death rate as 90 per 1000 on the Blood and Peigan Reserves in 1900. He infers most of it was from "tuberculosis rife among them".

50 Leonard, D. — On the North Trail. The Treaty #8 Diary of O.C. Edwards, Publication #12, HSA 1999. Dr. Kennedy acknowledges Dr. Edwards' interest in the medical registration system, and his contribution to the formation of the NWT Medical Association and drafting of its first bylaws in 1889. In 1906 Edwards became the first registrant of the new Alberta College of Physicians and Surgeons. Dr. Kennedy became the fifteenth.

51 Kerr, W.J. — Frank Slide, pages 18-26, 1990. Also see Frank Anderson's Tragedies of the Crows Nest Pass, pages 38-39. Heritage House, 1999.

52 Mewburn, F.H. — The Life and Work of Dr. George A. Kennedy, page 327. Dr. H.C. Jamieson indicates Dr. R.G. Brett was President of the Alberta Medical Association and the Alberta College in 1906/7. There were legal difficulties starting the College as recounted in Dr. Lampard's profile of Dr. J.D. Lafferty. For a more in depth discussion of "The Medical Profession the North West Territories" see Dr. Hilda Neatby's article in the CACHB 14(4): 61-77, February 1950. The CACHB republished the original article in Saskatchewan History 2(2), May 1949 but without references.

53 Learmonth, G.E. — The 50th Anniversary of the Alberta Medical Association, AMB 20(3): 51-57, August 1955. Confirmed in Heber Jamieson's Early Medicine in Alberta, pages 61-64, 201.

54 Kennedy, G.A. — Letter to the Editor of the Western Canadian Medical Journal on Dominion Registration, WCMJ 3: 34-35, January 1909. Dr. Kennedy noted the subject was a "hardy annual" one. He had been party to previous discussions on the issue of "reciprocity" in 1878. Scant attention to the Western Canadian initiative is given in H.E. MacDermot's History of the CMA 1: 79-82, 1935 and in R.B. Kerr's History of the Medical Council of Canada. For a photograph of the "Federation's" founding members see H.C. Jamieson's Early Medicine in Alberta, opposite page 65. The photograph is dated 1907, which is correct.
For a supportive reply see Manitoba's James Patterson's letter in the WCJM 3: 80-81, 1909 (n.d. circa January). He proposed Kennedy assume the role of a "western" Roddick. That idea evolved into a committee of Drs. Kennedy and Brett (AB) as well as Drs. Patterson and Milroy (MN). The four visited BC to gain a prairie consensus for a regional (Western) reciprocal medical examination and registration system, before the August 23-25 CMA convention in Winnipeg. The circular that was sent to the BC physicians is reprinted in WCJM 3(8): 368-370. Drs. Braithwaite, Kennedy and Brett attended the Saskatchewan Medical Association meeting and with difficulty gained their support, as recorded in Dr. E.A. Braithwaite's letter to Dr. G.R. Johnson, June 19, 1942, deposited in Glenbow in the Johnson Fonds, M600, File 2.

55 Brett, R.G. — Dr. Brett gave an address in the medical library at the Manitoba Medical College entitled, "Some aspects of the medical profession in the west", February 20, 1909, WCJM 3: 112-120, 126, 127, 1909.

56 Kerr, R.B. — The History of Medical Council of Canada, pages 14-23, 26, opp 66, 101 and Appendix B, MCC, 1979. Dr. Kennedy was appointed by the Governor in Council to the first MCC board in 1912. He was granted license #14. Dr. Braithwaite replaced him after his death in 1913. For Roddick's original MCC proposal see the Montreal Medical Journal, pages 1-6, April 1899. Dr. Roddick was appointed the Honourary President of the CMA for the rest of his life at the CMA convention in August 1912 in Edmonton for his contributions to the passage of the Canadian Medical "Roddick" Act in 1912. It created the MCC. Retiring CMA President Dr. H.G. Mackid of Calgary called for the motion; which was drowned out by a chorus of cheers.

57 Johns, W.H. — A History of the University of Alberta 1908-1969, page 15, 1970. Also see H.C. Jamieson's Early Medicine in Alberta, pages 101-102. For confirmation of his resignation in early 1909 see WCJM 3(6): 332-333, June 1909.

58 Stanley, G.D. — George Allan Kennedy, pages 7-10.

59 Kennedy, G.A. — The Battle at Belly River, pages 2-9. 2nd edition, Lethbridge Historical Society, 1968. Also see J.D. Higinbotham's When the West was Young, page 317. The Literary and Scientific Society (at Fort Macleod) was formed on December 14, 1884. C.A. Magrath assisted Kennedy with the maps and sketches as called in the Galts, Father and Son and How Alberta Grew Up, pages 32-33, circa 1929. Copy in the possession of the Galt Museum, Lethbridge.

60 Kennedy, G.A. — Fort Macleod - Our Colorful Past, pages 34, 43, 51, 66, 82, 95, 103, 1977. The "Kennedy Cup" for golf medal play was presented to the AMA by Dr. E.A. Braithwaite on behalf of Dr. A.H.N. Kennedy, as a memorial to Dr. Kennedy's father. The presentation was made at the CMA Alberta Division annual meeting on September 8, 1937. The first winner was Dr. H. Niewches in 1937.

61 Haultain, H. — NWMP Memories of a Doctor's Wife 1890-1904, page 140. Henrietta was Mrs. (Dr.) C.S. Haultain. The memoir was written circa 1938 and was deposited at Glenbow, M8538, File 46. Dr. deVeber visited the Kennedy home as the Game Warden, the day after Dr. Kennedy had shot and skinned the antelope out of season. While both laughed it off, it still cost Dr. Kennedy $25.

62 Learmonth, G.E. — The 50th Anniversary of the Alberta Medical Association. AMB 20(3): 51-57, August 1955. Dr. Learmonth first met Dr. Kennedy in Fort Macleod in 1903. He described him as "then approaching his prime of life...I was to meet him in subsequent years at meetings of the Alberta Medical Association, where he took a prominent part, especially in the 1906 organization meeting, of the Alberta Medical Association".

63 Mewburn, F.H. — The Life and Work of George A. Kennedy. Read before the Calgary Medical Society, February 7, 1928. CMAJ 21: 327-330, 1929. In Mewburn's introduction he regretted that no data has been collected on the "galaxy of Manitoba Men" that he found on his arrival in Winnipeg in 1882. He hoped that by presenting and authoring the Life and Work of Dr. Kennedy, more would follow. The Calgary Medical Society (CMS) was organized c1906. CMS minutes in the file at the Glenbow archives do not start until 1928. The only other documented CMS presentation on an early Alberta doctor was by Dr. R.G. Brett on Dr. H.G. Mackid in 1928. No notes or published papers have been located in the Glenbow Museum or Brett archives in Banff, on this presentation. Both Drs. Mewburn and Brett passed away in 1929.

64 Jamieson, H.C. — Early Medicine in Alberta, page 189. Alan joined his father in practice and registered with the Alberta College in 1908. He died at age 65 in 1954. Mrs. (G.A.) Alice Maud Kennedy died in 1936. AMB 1: 33, April 1936. Ethel Francis' birth year was deduced from Dr. George Kennedy's biography in A.O. MacRae's History of Alberta II: 679 and J.D. Higinbotham's, When the West Was Young, page 318.

65 Kennedy, G.A. — Obituary, CMAJ 3: 1016, 1913.

66 Kennedy, G.A. — Obituary, Macleod Spectator (Gazette), Oct. 9, 1913.

67 Kerr, R.B. — The History of the Medical Council of Canada, pages 20-23, 26, opp 66, and 101-113, MCC, 1970. Dr. Kennedy was registrant #14 of the MCC; Dr. Brett #6 and Dr. Park #23. The first 32 registrants were the members on the MCC Board. Licenses were issued in alphabetical order except for Dr. Roddick's which was #1. The first Board meeting was held November 7-9, 1912 in Ottawa. The Board stood for the first photo in front of the original parliament buildings in Ottawa. The first annual MCC meeting was held June 17-19, 1913. The Register was opened July 1, 1913 and the first examinations were conducted October 7-9, 1913. Dr. Kennedy, along with Dr. W.T. Baptie (BC) and Dr. T.G. Roddick were the first 3 appointees by the Governor in Council (Federal Cabinet), giving credence to Dr. Pattersons remark in the WCMJ February, 1909 that Kennedy was the "Western Roddick".

68 LaDow, B. — The Medicine Line. Life and Death on a North American Borderland. Pages 40-42, Routledge, 2002. Hugh Dempsey says Indians interpreted the "Imaginary line" as having magical differences, when viewed from one side of the border or the other. Also see Turner in "Across the Medicine Line", pages 19, 36, 222, M&S, 1973.

69 Stanley, G.A. — George Allan Kennedy, AMB 16(3): 45, August 1955. A tablet to his memory was placed in the Fort Macleod Anglican Church.

Dr. Leverett George deVeber

1 Campbell, P.M. — The Life of L.G. deVeber, Alberta Medical Bulletin 14(3): 43-44, July 1949.

2 Campbell, P.M. — Obituary, Leverett George deVeber, CMAJ 15: 971, 1925. Dr. deVeber always signed his name L. Geo. DeVeber. The family prefer the deVeber spelling of the name.

3 deVeber, G. — Personal communication with Dr. George deVeber, L.G.'s grandson, May 6, 2004.

4 MacRae, A.O. — Leverett George deVeber MD History of the Province of Alberta, pages 783-784, 1912. Other birth dates given are Feb. 11 and Feb. 15, 1849. The deVeber family have confirmed the Feb. 10 date.

5 Campbell, P.M. — The life of L.G. deVeber, pages 43-44.

6 Blue, J. — Leverett George deVeber, MD, Alberta Past and Present, III: 267-269, Pioneer Historical Publishing, 1924.

7 Campbell, P.M. — The Life of L.G. deVeber, page 44.

8 Blue, J. — Leverett George deVeber, page 268. John Blue indicates Dr. deVeber was in practice in New Brunswick for six years before joining the NWMP. All other references (CMAJ obituary, Lethbridge Herald Death Notice, A.O. MacRae and G.M. McDougall's Medical Clinics and Physicians in Southern Alberta) are silent on the question.

9 Campbell, P.M. — The Life of L.G. deVeber, page 44.

10 Stanley, G.D. — Hon. L.G. deVeber, CACHB 2(1): 11-12, May 1937.

11 Stanley, G.D. — Honourable L.G. deVeber, pages 11-12. Also see Gordon E. Tolton's, The Rocky Mountain Rangers, page 44.

12 Kennedy, G.A. — "Report of Surveyor (sic) Kennedy', Fort Macleod, 4 Dec 1882. Appended to the NWMP Annual Report for 1882. Reprinted in Settlers and Rebels, pages 32-33, Coles Canadiana, 1973.

13 (deVeber, L.G.) — Five Terrible Days and Nights: a Mounted Policeman Gets Snow blinded and Is Lost a Horse's Instinct Saves his Life. Fort Macleod Gazette, April 14, 1883. "Parker...is now...under Dr. deVeber's care, who will no doubt bring him around". Alberta History 5(15): 5, Autumn 1957.

14 Stanley, G.D. — Honourable L.G. deVeber, page 12. The distance is variously given as 130, 167, 170, 187 miles. Four or five horses were used. Dr. Stanley's account was based on a reply from Mrs. deVeber, then living in Ottawa. Also see P.M. Campbell's Obituary; G.M. McDougall's Medical Clinics and Physicians of Southern Alberta, pages 114-115; and The Pioneer Pemmican Club Roundup 1885-1985, page 92, Galt Museum.

15 Campbell, P.M. — Obituary, Leverett George DeVeber, CMAJ, 15:971, 1925. Also see G.E. Learmonth CMAJ 15: 868, 1925.

16 Kells, E. — Pioneer Interview with Mrs. deVeber (n.d.), pages 9, 10, circa 1935. Copy deposited in Glenbow, 1960.

17 Trew, D.E. — "An Early Pioneer' as related by the late Rachel Frances deVeber. 8 pages. No date but circa 1947. Deposited in the Alberta Legislative Library, Edmonton.

18 deVeber, L.G. — NWMP discharge documents, dated February 11, 1885 at Regina, NWT.

19 deVeber, B. — Personal communication, August 17, 2004.

20 Tolton, Gordon E. — The Rocky Mountain Rangers, pages 43, 44, 50, 68-69, 86. Occasional Paper #28, Lethbridge Historical Society, 1994.

21 Dempsey, H.A. — Rocky Mountain Rangers. Alberta History 5(2): 3-6, Spring 1957.

22 Higinbotham, J.D. — Letter to Dr. P.M. Campbell, February 18, 1930.

23 Stanley, G.D. — Herbert Rimington Meade, CACHB 6(3): 10-14, November 1941.

24 (deVeber, L.G.) — Fort Macleod: Our Colorful Past, pages 43, 65, 216, 433-435, 1975.

25 Jamieson, H.C. — Early Medicine in Alberta, page 43, AMA, 1947.

26 (deVeber, L.G.) — Lethbridge Herald April 12, 1960 reprinted May 28, 1991. Also see the Macleod Gazette of April 9, 1891.

27 Johnston, A., et al — Lethbridge Its Medical Doctors, Dentists, Drug Stores, Occasional Paper #24, pages 6, 19, 24, 32, Lethbridge Historical Society, 1991.

28 Johnston, A., et al — Lethbridge Its Medical Doctors, Dentists, Drug Stores, pages 70, 71.

29 (deVeber, L.G.) — Report 6(3): 10-14, November 1941 to the Chairman Health and Relief Committee, Town of Lethbridge, for April 1898, by the Medical Officer of Health. Jamieson suggests deVeber's appointment started in 1893.

30 (deVeber, L.G.) — Letter from John A. Rew, Clerk, (NWT) Executive Council to B. Bowman Secretary-Treasurer, Lethbridge, August 10, 1898. Copy in the deVeber family archives.

31 Neatby, H. — The Medical Profession in the North West Territories, Saskatchewan History 2(2): 1-15, Spring 1949.

32 (deVeber, L.G.) — MOH Reports 1898-1901. Copies in the deVeber family archives.

33 Higinbotham, J.D. — When the West was Young, pages 247-248, Ryerson 1933.

34 (deVeber, L.G.) — Correspondence dated October 3, 10, 24, 26, 1905, in the deVeber Family Archives.

35 Babcock, D.R. — Alexander Cameron Rutherford, A Gentleman of Strathcona, pages 26-29, UofC Press, 1989.

36 Fairbairn, J. — "The Canadian Senate" in Lethbridge Historical Society Newsletter #4, July 1992. Also see G.M. McDougall's Medical Clinics and Physicians of Southern Alberta, page 100 and D.R. Babcock's Alexander Cameron Rutherford, pages 26-31, 149-154, UofC, 1989.

37 (deVeber, L.G.) — Lethbridge Herald April 12, 1906, reprinted May 28, 1991.

38 Blue, J. — Leverett George deVeber MD, page 269.

39 McDougall, G.M. — Medical Clinics and Physicians in Southern Alberta, pages 98-100, UofC, 1991. Also see P.M. Campbell's The Life of L.G. deVeber, AMB 14(3): 43-44, July 1949.

40 Campbell, P.M. — The Life of L.G. deVeber, page 44.

41 deVeber, L.G. — Few Congratulatory Remarks. Speech to the (Lethbridge) Nursing Graduating Class, (n.d.) post 1913. Deposited in the deVeber family archives in possession of Dr. George deVeber, Dr. L.G. deVeber's grandson.

42 Johnston, A., et al — Lethbridge: Its Medical Doctors, Dentists, Drug Stores, pages 19-20.

43 Aubrey, M.K. — Letter to R. Lampard, April 30, 2002. Ms. Aubrey was the Head of the Geographic Names Program, Alberta Government. The Senators were Hardisty, Talbot, deVeber, Forget, Cote and Lougheed. Dr. Roy was the only Senator omitted. Mt. Lougheed was "moved" one year later in 1926, ostensibly because it couldn't be seen from the CPR. Details of Mt. deVeber are recorded in Pat Holmgren's 2000 Place Names in Alberta, pages 44-45, 1972.

44 Cautley, R.W., Wheeler, A.O. — Report of the Commission Appointed to Delimit the Boundary between the Provinces of Alberta and British Columbia Part III, pages 33-35, 62, Ottawa, 1925. The reconnaissance "station" was named "deVeber" in 1922.

45 Veitch, A. — deVebers make first assault on the Peak with their name on it. The Grand Cache Mountaineer, August 27, 2002.

Dr. Frank Hamilton Mewburn

1 Rawlinson, H.E. — Frank Hamilton Mewburn, Canadian Journal of Surgery 2:1-5, October 1958.

2 Bishop, W.J. — The Early History of Surgery, pages 172-181, Robert Hale 1960.

In 1880 Spencer Wells published his 1858-1880 series of 1000 ovariotomies (a complete or wedge resection, of the ovary). It was the largest series of intra-abdominal operations to that date. It was followed by the first cholecystectomy (1882), and the first successful ectopic pregnancy operation, by Lawson Tait in 1883. By 1882, Willard Parker had performed 80 operations to remove perityphlic (periappendicular) abscesses from 1867-1882. These cases were thought to arise from a rare disease called a perforated appendix (1884), as confirmed at postmortem. The term "appendicitis" and the dangers of perforation, were not described until 1885 by R.H. Fitz of Boston. Early surgery for appendicitis was not recommended until 1886, by H.B. Sands. The first planned appendectomy for appendicitis, was performed by McBurney in 1889, in which he described McBurney's point of abdominal sensitivity over the appendix. McBurney's abdominal muscle splitting procedure to reduce postoperative hernias, was not detailed until 1894.

For a discussion of early Western Canadian surgery, medicine, physicians and hospitals see:

1) In Manitoba: I. Carr and R.E. Beamish's Manitoba Medicine - a Brief History, pages 23-34, UofM Press, 1999; and N.T. McPhedran's The Development of Surgery in Western Canada in the Prairie Medical Journal 67(1): 55-59, Spring 1997.

2) In Saskatchewan: C.S. Houston's Dr. M.M. Seymour, Annals of the RCPSC 31(1): 41-43, February 1998; Joan Feather's Hospitals in Saskatchewan in Territorial Days in Saskatchewan History 40(2): 62-71, Spring 1987; and L.H. Thomas' Early Territorial Hospitals, Saskatchewan History 2(2):16-20, Spring 1949.

3) In Alberta: H.C. Jamieson's Early Medicine in Alberta, pages 17-37 (NWMP and CPR eras), 88-100 (Hospitals), AMA 1947; and Janet Ross-Kerr's Prepared to Care, pages 17-20, UofA 1998.

3 Mackid, H.G. — The Presidents Address at the Annual Meeting of the Association at Edmonton August 10, 1912. CMAJ 2(9): 801-811, September 1912. Dr. Mackid concluded his speech with the rhetorical question, "What is the value of the West to Medicine?" and provided the answer, "Does not the answer lie in the words, energy and newness and opportunity".

4 Higinbotham, J.D. — When the West Was Young, pages 156-174, Ryerson, 1933. Privately reprinted by Bruce Haig in 1978. Also see A.L.S. Peat's "19th Century Lethbridge", Occasional Paper #8, pages 37, 40, Lethbridge Historical Society 1978.

5 den Otter, A.A. — Urban Pioneers of Lethbridge. Alberta History 25 (1): 15-24, Winter 1977.

6 Mewburn, F.H. — The Life and Work of Dr. George Kennedy. CMAJ 21: 327-330, 1929.

7 Jamieson, H.C. — "Early Doctors in Southern Alberta", CMAJ 38: 391-397, 1938. Also see G.D. Stanley's Medical Pioneering in Alberta CACHB 1(3): 8, November 1936 and H.C. Jamieson's Early Medicine, pages 24-25, AMA 1947. For a more detailed account see W. Canniff's The Medical Profession in Upper Canada, pages 111, 511-515, 518, 1894, reprinted by Associated Medical Services (Hannah) in 1980; H.E. MacDermot's History of the Canadian Medical Association I: 135-136, CMA; and H.E. Rawlinson's Frank Hamilton Mewburn Canadian Journal of Surgery 2: 1-5, October 1958. The certificates, etc. are held in the UofA Archives, and are available on the UofA website.

8 Arnold, H.A. — Frank Hamilton Mewburn. Pioneer Surgeon of the West, 12 page manuscript. A paper read to the Fort Whoop Up (Lethbridge) Chapter of the Historical Society of Alberta, April 29, 1975. Published in the Lethbridge Historical Society Newsletter #6, pages 2-4, November 1991.

9 Brighty, K. — History of Nursing in Alberta 1942. The History of Nursing Questionnaire for the University of Alberta Hospital and School of Nursing, pages 1-2. Completed by Helen S. Peters, Superintendent of Nurses, February 8, 1940. Also see Janet Ross-Kerr's Prepared to Care, pages 158-159, UofA Press, 1998.

10 MacDermot, H.E. — Sir Thomas Roddick, pages 31-44, Macmillan, 1938. Also see Charles Roland's The Early Years of Antiseptic Surgery in Canada, pages 237-254 in Medicine in Canadian Society, McGill Queens 1981; and H.A. Arnold's Frank Hamilton Mewburn pages 4-5, for further elaboration on Listerian antisepsis and Mewburn's acceptance of and reflections on it.

11 Rawlinson, H.E. — Frank Hamilton Mewburn, Canadian Journal of Surgery 2: 1-5, October 1958.

12 MacDermot, H.E. — Sir Thomas Roddick, pages 45-83.

13 Rawlinson, H.E. — Frank Hamilton Mewburn, page 2. A photo of the four interns is dated 1882. Also see Elizabeth McCrum's Abstract of the UofA medical holdings, pages 12-13, 1980.

14 Board of Trustees — Report of the Secretary-Treasurer from April 1, 1882 to December 31, 1883, Winnipeg General Hospital (WGH); Minutes WGH November 11, 1884. Edith Patterson's Tales of Early Manitoba from the Winnipeg Free Press, pages 89-94, WFP, 1970. Dr. Mewburn succeeded Dr. L.J. Munro who left the WGH and moved to Edmonton, as it had no physicians. Munro practiced there until 1886.

15 Bergin, D. — The Medical and Surgical History of the Canadian North-West Rebellion of 1885, John Lovell and son, 1886, pages 20-22 (Kerr), 40-41 (Bell), 41-43 (Roddick). Also see H.E. MacDermot's "Roddick's

Work in the Riel Rebellion" in Sir Thomas Roddick, pages 45-68, Macmillan, 1938.

16 Lampard, R. — For a discussion of the 81 cases admitted to WGH including 17 transferred by barge from Saskatoon to the WGH in July 1885, and the medical services during the Riel Rebellion, see Letters to the Editor, CMAJ 154: 1624-5, June 1, 1996 and CMAJ: 155: 1392-1395, November 15, 1996 by Messrs Lampard, McCulloch and Rickman. Also see H.E. MacDermot's Sir Thomas Roddick, page 55; D. Bergin's Medical and Surgical History, page 20; Ross Mitchell's Manitoba Surgical Pioneers, CJS 3: 282-283, July 1960; Ethel Johns and Beatrice Fines, The WGH School of Nursing, pages 7-9, 1988.

Dr. Kerr, the first Dean of the Manitoba Medical College from 1882-1887 left the MMC and WGH for a post as the head of surgery at a medical school in Washington, DC. There he performed the first cholecystectomy and intussusception reduction. He had already operated on the son of a colleague in Winnipeg and had successfully reduced the boy's intussusception.

17 Bergin, D. — The Medical and Surgical History of the Canadian North-West Rebellion, pages 20-22. Report of Surgeon - Major James Kerr, April 16, 1886.

18 MacDermot, H.E. — Sir Thomas Roddick, pages 76-77, 83 and Dr. Bergin's Medical and Surgical History, pages 20-21.

19 Johns, E., & Fines, B. — WGH School of Nursing, pages 3-9, Centennial Edition 1988. The Winnipeg hospitals increased from 20 beds (1872) to 72 beds (1884).

20 Carr, I., & Beamish, R.E. — Medicine in Manitoba, pages 28-30, 1999. The authors note the first recorded operation in Manitoba was a lithotomy performed by Dr. J.A. O'Donnell in 1875. The first abdominal operation at WGH, they record as being performed by Dr. H.H. Chown in 1886. This is inconsistent with Dr. Hugh A. Arnold, who quotes Dr. Mewburn as saying he had seen two or three abdominal operations before he left the WGH in early 1886.

A sampling of contemporary British surgical experience was presented at the 57th annual meeting of the BMA and was summarized in the Northern Lancet, pages 54-56, 1889. A series of 248 intra-abdominal operations with 17 deaths from 1890-1897 was reported by Dr. A.L. Smith of Montreal in the (newly renamed) Winnipeg and Western Canada Lancet, pages 217-219, 1897. In his paper Dr. Smith concluded the surgical management of tubal pregnancy was one of the most brilliant advances in abdominal surgery that had been made. He presented 7 cases, all of whom recovered. Mewburn had already done his first ectopic pregnancy operation and reported on it in the Montreal Medical Journal, pages 3-4, February 1893. She died.

21 Braithwaite, E.A. — Early Days of the NWMP, pages 13, 28. Manuscript deposited in the Glenbow archives, Calgary. Reprinted as Reminiscences of a Hospital Sergeant, Alberta History 39: 15-25, Winter 1991. Braithwaite joined the NWMP in 1884. He served in the NW Rebellion and completed his medical training, receiving his MD from the Manitoba Medical College in 1890.

22 Johnston, A. — Lethbridge Its Medical Doctors, Dentists, Drug Stores, page 5, Lethbridge Historical Society Occasional Paper #24, 1991. Johnston indicates Mewburn arrived in January 1886.

23 Hogan, D.B. — Osler Goes West. Annals RCPSC 33(5): 316-319, August 2000. The party of six (Messrs. Wm. Osler, E.B. Osler, Barnes, Briggs, Burns and Peter White, MP) were in Winnipeg August 10. They took a side trip for 2 days on the incomplete M&NW (Portage la Prairie to Prince Albert) railway, during which time a lady delivered a baby in the (fortunately stationary) train toilet, which Osler was called upon to examine. He found the newborn bruised but uninjured, giving rise to his "obstetrical" reputation. The party arrived in Lethbridge, August 15. Their private railway car, compliments of the CPR's T.P. Shaughnessy, must have been sent to Calgary as the Galt Railway was a narrow gauge one. The party was in Fort Macleod on the 16th and Calgary on the 18th, camping by a lake on the way. This visit likely gives rise to Dr. Kennedy's (last) "typhomalaria" research request for a "collective investigation...(of the fever with) records...properly classified and worked up...ought to be possible...to found...a treatise..." See Assistant Surgeon Kennedy's annual NWMP Report for 1886. His senior, Dr. A. Jukes, whose family was well known to Dr. Osler, declined. For the reference to Kennedy's disappointment, see Mewburn's Life and Work of Dr. G.A. Kennedy, pages 327-328. Mewburn notes in his 1886 NWMP report from Lethbridge "One death is recorded due to typhoid fever, which was in all probability contracted in Battleford'. Mewburn was not equivocal in his diagnosis. See NWMP Report for 1886, Appendix W. pages 107-108, Coles Canadiana, 1973.

24 Arnold, H.A. — Frank Hamilton Mewburn, page 7.

25 Johnston, A. et al — Lethbridge: Its Medical Doctors, Dentists, Drug Stores, page 32. The first OR was in Fort Macleod and was built by the NWMP, in 1884. The second was built in Banff circa 1887 by Dr. R.G. Brett. The first public hospital with an OR was built in Medicine Hat in 1889. Dr. Brett of Banff was performing major abdominal surgery in his OR in Banff by 1892. See R. Lampard's Dr. R.G. Brett, Alberta History 51(2): 15, Spring 2003 and E.A. Braithwaite's Early Days, page 24.

26 Mewburn, F.H. — Case of Tubal-Pregnancy. Montreal Medical Journal, pages 3-4, February 1893. Dr. L.G. deVeber had moved to Lethbridge

and was giving anesthetics for Dr. Mewburn by 1891. See A. Johnston et al, pages 6, 32.

27 Braithwaite, E.A. — Edmonton Journal, February 18, 1946.

28 Deane, R.B. — Mounted Police Life in Canada, pages 44-48, Cassel, 1916.

29 Jamieson, H.C. — Early Medicine in Alberta, page 91, AMA 1947.

30 Stanley, G.D. — Medical archives and their relation to the profession, CACHB 15(2): 28-35, August 1950. Also see H.C. Jamieson Early Medicine, pages 90-91 and Francis Coulson's Frank Hamilton Mewburn, page 125. She refers to Dr. Mewburn as the "First Surgeon in the West".

31 Coulson, F.S. — "The First Surgeon in the West": Frank Hamilton Mewburn: 1858-1929", CACHB 10(2): 120-125, 1945. Frances Coulson was the daughter of a Lethbridge physician, who worked with Dr. Mewburn about 1910. She was also an avocational-historian in the Calgary Associate Clinic. Also see Dr. Hugh A. Arnold's manuscript on Frank Hamilton Mewburn, page 9 and P. Campbell's Frank Hamilton Mewburn, CACHB 15(4): 65, 1951.

32 Chatenay, H. — Country Doctors, page 11, Matrix Press 1980. Also see G.D. Stanley's CACHB 21(1): 21, May 1956.

33 Galbraith, W.S. — Frank Hamilton Mewburn: Appreciations, CMAJ 20: 329, 1929.

34 Higinbotham, J.D. — When the West was Young, page 170. Higinbotham agreed with Dr. Galbraith. So does Dr. H.E. Rawlinson in Frank Hamilton Mewburn, page 4; as does Alex Johnston in Lethbridge Its Medical Doctors, Dentists and Drug Stores, page 5. A comparison of dates and times, with the milestones recorded in W.J. Bishops the Early History of Surgery, page 172-181 (reference #1), confirms Galbraith et al as correct. Dr. N.T. McPhedran, a former Professor and Head of Surgery at the UofC, comments that appendicitis was well known, but still often not diagnosed until an abscess formed in the right lower quadrant. The treatment then was to drain the abscess. This "delayed treatment" carried considerable hazards. Prairie Medical Journal 67(1):57, Spring 1997.

35 Galbraith, Walter S. — Frank Hamilton Mewburn, page 329. J.D. Higinbotham notes Mewburn performed countless hernias in When the West was Young, page 170. Mewburn is unnamed as the surgeon, when Theodore Brandley perforated his gallbladder, he placed his faith and trust in the Lord and "the young surgeons who had never witnessed a gallstone operation". After surgery in October 1901 Brandley slowly recovered, though a sinus tract must have developed as it discharged for the next 25 years. See Alberta History 9(3): 23-29, Summer 1961.

36 Rawlinson, H.E. — Frank Hamilton Mewburn, page 4.

37 Jamieson, H.C. — Early Medicine In Alberta, page 91-92. Also see the Western Canadian Medical Journal 2(3): 105-113, 271, 1908 (Appendicitis, a plead for early operation) and 4:451-456, 1910 (Surgery's Balance Sheet). The mortality ratio varied from three to one hundred percent, depending on the surgical procedure used, the severity of the case, the surgeon's judgement and experience, and patient's consent.

38 Scarlett, E.P. — Eastern Gate and Western Cavalcade: McGill men in Western Canada, CACHB 21(1): 18-19, May 1956.

39 Feather, J. — Hospitals in Saskatchewan in Territorial Days, Saskatchewan History 40(2): 62-71, Spring 1987; and C.S. Houston's Maurice MacDonald Seymour: A Leader in Public Health, Annals of the RCPSC 31(1): 41-43, February 1998.

A new hospital of 25 beds was built for the 250 NWMP in Regina in 1887. No surgery/dispensary or drug storage rooms were included in the plans, so 10 beds (2 wards) on the main floor were used for these purposes. In Dr. A. Jukes NWMP report from Regina for 1887, he records 2 clavicular fractures and 1 inguinal hernia, all treated conservatively; and 1 large scalp "tumor" as "operated on", presumably by an incision and drainage. For Dr. Augustus Jukes NWMP Report for 1887, see pages 98-104 in Law and Order, Coles Canadiana, 1973.

40 Edwards, G.E., & Harkness, D.B. — Life Near the Bone, pages 15-21, 163-164, 166, privately printed, 1991.

41 Johnston, A. — Lethbridge, Its Medical Doctors, Dentists, Drug Stores, pages 9, 32, 41, Occasional Paper 24, Lethbridge Historical Society 1991.

42 Mewburn, F.H. — The Life and Work of Dr. George A. Kennedy, page 329.

43 Coulson, F.S. — "The First Surgeon in the West", page 123. Another early case in which Mewburn was secondarily involved, was a wound exploration on Fort Macleod lawyer C.C. McCaul. Two months before the operation McCaul had a gun accident, resulting in a penetrating wound of his chest. Dr. Kennedy, using hindsight, didn't think the surgery should have been performed, as he described in the Canadian Practitioner, pages 377-379, December 1888. The patient survived until 1928 or age 71. See Mewburn's The Life and Work of Dr. George A. Kennedy, page 329 and A.D. Ridge's C.C. McCaul, Pioneer Lawyer, Alberta History 21(1): 21-25, 1973.

44 Campbell, Peter M. — "Frank Hamilton Mewburn", Calgary Associate Clinic Historical Bulletin 15(4): 61-69, February 1951.

45 Campbell, Peter M. — Frank Hamilton Mewburn, page 65.

46 Learmonth, G.E. — The Fiftieth Anniversary of the Alberta Medical Association, AMB 20(3): 54, 1955.

47 Learmonth, G.E. — The Fiftieth Anniversary, pages 51-57. Also see Dr.

G.D. Stanley's The NWT Medical Association, CACHB 16(2): 38-39, August 1951.

48 Jamieson, H.C. — Early Medicine, pages 53-54, 201.

49 MacDermot, H.E. — The History of the Canadian Medical Association II: 3, 1958. Also see H.C. Jamieson's Early Medicine, pages 72-73 and A. Schartner's Health Units of Alberta, pages 22-24, HUAA, 1982.

50 Mewburn, F.H. — Edmonton Journal, January 10, 1956.

51 Newsletter — Lethbridge Historical Society, page 3, No. 2, March 2, 2004. Mayor Mewburn asked Will and Harry Fairfield to start a nursery to supply trees for Lethbridge boulevards. They did.

52 Campbell, P.M. — Frank Hamilton Mewburn, page 68; F.S. Coulson's, The First Surgeon in the West, page 124. Dr. Mewburn wasn't always so financially successful. See R.B. Deane's Mounted Police Life in Canada, page 72.

53 Editor — Calgary General Hospital 1890-1955, 65 Years of Community Services, page 20, 1955. Dr. H.G. Mackid also received his Fellowship in the American College of Surgeons in the first year, 1913, but unfortunately had developed diabetes in 1910. Personal communication S. Rishworth, archivist American College of Surgeons, November 25, 2003. His friend of 27 years, Dr. G. A. Kennedy developed a soon to be fatal oral cancer in early 1913.

54 MacRae, A.O. — History of the Province of Alberta I: 578-579, 1912.

55 Campbell, P.M. — Frank Hamilton Mewburn, page 63. Also see Dr. G.D. Stanley's Medical Archives and their Relation to the Profession, CACHB 15(2): 32, August 1950, and H.E. Rawlinson's, Frank Hamilton Mewburn, page 4.

56 Mewburn, F.H. — WWI Military records: Record of Promotions, etc. Reference RG 150, Box 6145-70, National Archives of Canada. Dr. Mewburn's second posting to the CAMC Medical Depot at Shorncliffe (March 10-April 17, 1917), overlapped with the first month Dr. E.G. Mason was permanently posted to the Depot. The large Shorncliffe base was under the overall command of General (Sir) Sam Steele. For dates see the Dr. E.G. Mason profile.

57 Lampard, R. — Profile of Dr. E.G. Mason. Desmond Martin wrote, Military Medicine and State Medicine, pages 52-53, in C.D. Naylor's Medical Care and the State, McGill Queens, 1992, that senior medical officers were suspected of abusing their perquisites for pleasure or profit. No date(s) are given.

58 Macbeth, R.A. — Alexander Russel Munroe, Canadian Journal of Surgery 10: 3-10, January 1967. Other surgeons under his command included Captains R.M. Janes the future Head of Surgery at UofT; Captain A. Grant Fleming the future Dean of Medicine at McGill and Dr. Alexander Munroe who succeeded Dr. Mewburn as the Head of Surgery at UofA in 1929.

59 Coulson, F.S. — First Surgeon in the West: Frank Hamilton Mewburn, page 124.

60 Edwards, G.E., & Harkness, D.B. — Life Near the Bone, page 20, as quoted from an address to the Calgary Medical Society by Dr. R.B. Deane in 1921. The manuscript is in the possession of Audrey Manning.

61 Vant, R., & Cashman, T. — More Than a Hospital, page 66, UAH, 1986. Also see A.C. Rankin's The Provincial Medical School, AMB 1(2): 7-11, 1935 and E.A. Corbet's Frontiers of Medicine, pages 29-33, UofA, 1990. The Mewburn's bought a house, where the AMA and College offices later stood at 9901-108th Street. Dr. D.R. Wilson recalls delivering their newspaper and how Dr. Mewburn kept his horse in the back yard. (Personal Communication Dr. R.A. Burns, Registrar, Alberta College of Physicians and Surgeons December 11, 2003).

62 McGugan, A.C. — History of the University of Alberta Hospital, pages 8, 22, UAH, 1964. Also see R. Vant and T. Cashman's More Than a Hospital, page 69, UAH, 1986.

63 Brighty, K. — History of Nursing in Alberta 1942. History of Nursing Questionnaire for the University of Alberta Hospital and School of Nursing, pages 1-2. Completed by Helen S. Peters, Superintendent of Nurses, February 8, 1940. Also see Janet Ross-Kerr's Prepared to Care, pages 158-159, UofA, 1998.

64 Wilson, B. — To Teach this Art, pages 43-44, 1977.

65 Vant, R., & Cashman, T. — As quoted in More Than a Hospital, pages 66-69 and P.M. Campbell's Frank Hamilton Mewburn, CACHB 15(4): 61-69. Also see J.D. Higinbotham pages 163, 169, 171-172; G.D. Stanley CACHB 15(2): 30-33; H.E. Rawlinson pages 4-5; H.C. Jamieson's Early Medicine page 91; E.P. Scarlett CACHB 21(1): 20-21, May 1956; T. Cashman's Heritage of Service page 37, 1966; B. Wilson's To Teach this Art pages 43-44, 103, 1977; L. Poelman's White Caps and Red Roses pages 2-6, circa 1980; C.A. Magrath's The Galts n.d., page 29, circa 1929; E.A. Braithwaite's Early Days, page 33; G.E. Edwards and D.B. Harkness page 20.
Dr. Scarlett identified Drs. F.H. Mewburn, G.D. Stanley and Bob Edwards as the three most memorable figures in Alberta to 1935, in his Transcript of an Interview recorded by C.G. Roland and deposited in Glenbow, page 31, November 1978.

66 Stephenson, G.W. — American College of Surgeons at 75, page 172 ACS, 1994. Dr. Mewburn followed Drs. F.N.G. Starr (1924/5) and Dr. J.S. McEachern (1925/6) as the second Vice-President of the ACS.

67 Mewburn, F.H. — 1) "Case of Tubal Pregnancy". Montreal Medical Journal, pages 3-4, February 1893; 2) Observations on (about 200) Lesions of Peripheral Nerves, with special reference to pre-operative and post-operative treatment, Medical Quarterly, pages 279-294, October 1921. Presented to the Medical Society of the Witley Camp Area, the Epsom Society and the Medical Society, Calgary (n.d.). It closes with the comment "End result...statistics (on about 200 cases of peripheral nerve lesions) will appear later. The results so far obtained, however, have been such as to give great encouragement". No "end result" statistical reports have been found. 3) The Life and Work of Dr. George A. Kennedy CMAJ 21: 327-330, 1929 after presentation to the Calgary Medical Society February 7, 1928; 4) "Notes on the Re-organization of the Department of Surgery, University of Alberta", 1923. His son F.H.H. (Hank) Mewburn wrote a "Report of the Orthopedic Department, University of Alberta", in 1924.

68 Braithwaite, E.A. — Early Days, page 34.

69 Higinbotham, J.D. — When the West was Young, page 173.

70 Arnold, H.A. — Frank Hamilton Mewburn, page 8. Also see A.O. MacRae's History of Alberta II: 776, 1912. Helene became Mrs. Beverley Robinson of Toronto, Calgary Herald April 27, 1927.

71 Macbeth, R.A. — Personal communication May 23, 2003. The two Roberts (Macbeth, Mewburn) grew up together in Edmonton. The dynasty of seven generations of Mewburn doctors started in 1765 and ended in 1977. Nine certificates from 1765 to 1860 are held in the University of Alberta Archives in the Jamieson Papers Accession 81-104, 25/1/2 Box 4, #44 and Accession 76-95, #10. They have been scanned and are available on the UAA website. Dr. Macbeth has written the Dictionary of Canadian Biography insert on Dr. Mewburn.

71 Mewburn, F.H. — Obituaries and Appreciations by Dr. H.C. Jamieson, A.C. Rankin and W.S. Galbraith, CMAJ 20: 328-329, 1929.

73 Campbell, P.M. — Frank Hamilton Mewburn, page 69.

74 Rawlinson, H.E. — Frank Hamilton Mewburn, page 4. Also see the minutes of the Council of Physicians and Surgeons, December 19, 1913 and September 21, 1914. The College gave the Edmonton Academy of Medicine $500 for their library.

75 Rankin, A.C. — University of Alberta Faculty of Medicine, AMB 1(2): 7-11, 1935; E.A. Corbet's, Frontiers of Medicine opp. page 44 UofA 1990; and G.E. Edwards and D.B. Harkness' Life Near the Bone, page 35.

76 Editor — General News, Alberta Medical Bulletin, page 4, July 1937. Also see the Lethbridge Herald, June 10, 1937.

Dr. George Henry Malcolmson

1 McGuffin, W.H. — Address to the Canadian Association of Radiologists, March 4, 1939. As quoted in Henry Chatenay's The Century Doctors, page 17, Matrix Press, 1980.

2 Stanley, G.D. — Dr. George Malcolmson, CACHB 14(4): 78-85, February 1950. This comprehensive article on Dr. Malcolmson was written from notes made during a "recent" visit to Edmonton to meet with Dr. Malcolmson's widow, Dr. Pat Malcolmson and Dr. J.O. Baker. Other Edmontonians who knew Dr. Malcolmson added colorful comments. Also see the chapter on Dr. Malcolmson by Henry Chatenay in Country Doctors, pages 5-17, Matrix Press, 1980. H.C. Jamieson provided a paragraph on Dr. Malcolmson in Early Medicine in Alberta, page 131, AMA, 1947.

3 Stanley, G.D. — Doctors in Alberta registered for over 40 years. CACHB 8(4): 22, February 1944.

4 Stanley, G.D. — Dr. George Malcolmson, pages 78-79.

5 Smith, C.M. — Marion Moodie: from proper lady to new woman. Alberta History 49(1): 9-15, Winter 2001. Also see the Jamieson manuscript entitled Marion E. Moodie, first nurse to graduate in Alberta, deposited in the Heber C. Jamieson Papers accession #81-104 at the UofA Archives, 5 pages, (n.d.). Miss Moodie started her nursing career at the nine bed CGH in April 1895, three weeks before its five patients were moved to the second CGH. She was the first nurse to graduate in Alberta, in 1898. Miss Moodie spent the next five years doing private duty nursing throughout Southern Alberta. Catherine Munn Smith was a third generation CGH nurse. Ms. Moodie was her great-Aunt. The article is based on Ms. Moodie's autobiographical notes, which are undated and unreferenced as to location.

6 Anderson, F. — The Frank Slide Story. Frontier Book No. 1 pages 30, 32-33, 38, 42-55, 58. Frontiers Unlimited, Calgary, 1983.

7 Kerr, J.W. — Frank Slide, page 6, 1990.

8 Cruden, D.M. — Report on the Great Landslide at Frank, Alberta History 50(2): 16-21, Spring 2002.

9 Anderson, F. — The Frank Slide Story, page 47.

10 Kerr, J.W. — Frank Slide, pages 20, 26.

11 Anderson, F. — The Frank Slide Story, pages 32-33.

12 Kerr, J.W. — Frank Slide, pages 18, 21. The two photographs show two nurses at the doorway of the NWMP barracks and Miss Moodie with a patient. The latter appears to be in Dr. Malcolmson's living room. Injuries included a fractured thigh (Warrington), splinter penetrating the liver (Ackroyd), internal injuries (Watkins), shock (Watkins), scrapes and

bruises (six in the Ennis family), bruised leg (Warrington) and bruised chest (McKenzie).

13 Houston, C.S. — D.A. Stewart, 1874-1937: Western Tuberculosis Pioneer. Annals RCPSC 25(1): 36-38, February 1992. David Stewart returned to Frank in the summer of 1903 to do a locum. Dr. Stewart pioneered the TB program at the Ninette Sanitorium in Manitoba.

14 Stewart, D.A. — A Disaster in the Rockies. Canadian Magazine 1903(4): 227-233. The article is one of the most descriptive and well illustrated (9 photographs) of the Slide. The population of Frank was 1000.

15 Kerr, J.W. — Frank Slide, pages 14-15.

16 Anderson, F. — The Frank Slide Story, page 47.

17 Anderson, F. — The Frank Slide Story, pages 47-48. For a photo of the barracks see T.W. Kerr's Frank Slide, page 81.

18 McConnell, R.G., & Brock, R.W. — Report on the Great Landslide at Frank, Alberta, 1903, 52 pages, June 12, 1903. Geological Survey of Canada (GSC). The report was included as Part VIII of the 1903 GSE annual report and was reprinted by the Edmonton Geological Society in 2003. The report concluded that sudden movement, weather, earthquake shock, heavy precipitation, rapid temperature change, closing chambers of the mine "...may precipitate...a second destructive slide...It certainly seems advisable that it be moved a short distance up the valley...".

19 Stanley, G.D. — Dr. George Malcolmson, page 82. Stanley says Malcolmson decided to install an x-ray machine in 1906. Jamieson in Early Medicine in Alberta, page 131, says it arrived in 1907. Dr. E.A. Braithwaite brought his first x-ray unit to Edmonton in 1906. In his letter to Dr. G.R. Johnson June 19, 1942, Dr. Braithwaite is careful to point out that he brought the first, second and third x-ray machines to Edmonton, not Alberta.

20 Becker, A. — Radiological Pioneers in Saskatoon, Saskatchewan History 34(3): 31-37, Winter 1983. Also see the Braithwaite and Mackid profiles for a discussion of their early x-ray machines in 1906-8.

21 MacEwan, D. — The history of imaging in Manitoba. Prairie Medical Journal 66(2): 75-78, 1996.

22 Parsons, W.B. — Information on the Early Days of Radiology in Alberta (n.d.). The article was originally submitted to Dr. E.M. Crawford, Archivist for the Canadian Association of Radiologists (CAR). A copy was deposited in UAA as Manuscript #77-183-3. Dr. Parsons' cautions he could find no primary documentary material over a six month search. His sources were from conversations and letters he recorded (n.d.) sometime after 1959. An updated, abridged version of Parsons' article, dated 1974,

appeared in J. Aldrich and B. Lentle's "A New Kind of Ray" pages 157-163, CAR 1995. The earliest recorded use of an x-ray machine uncovered by Dr. Parsons, was in Medicine Hat, by Dr. Woodland. No date is given. The second unit Parsons records was purchased by Dr. Lovering in Lethbridge, sometime after 1909.

23 Letts, H. — The Edmonton Academy of Medicine: A History, page 5, Edmonton Academy, 1986. Stanley states the new RAH opened in 1911 (CACHB 14: 82), but Jamieson says it was in 1910 in Early Medicine, p131.

24 Jamieson, H.C. — Early Medicine in Alberta, pages 199, 201, AMA, 1947. Also see the WCMJ 2(9): 393, 1908. During Dr. Malcolmson's Alberta College of Physicians and Surgeons term in 1913/14, he chaired the committee that recommended the starting of library grants to the Edmonton Academy of Medicine. An extract of the college minutes of December 19, 1913, is located in the G.R. Johnson Fonds, File M600, File 6 in Glenbow.

25 Jamieson, H.C. — Early Medicine in Alberta, page 102.

26 Stanley, G.D. — Dr. George Malcolmson, page 85.

27 Letts, H. — The Edmonton Academy of Medicine: A History, page 5.

28 Hardwick, E., Jamieson, E., & Tregillus, E. — The Science, the Art and the Spirit, pages 81-86, Volume 4, Century Calgary, 1975. The authors erroneously suggest Dr. McGuffin's Radium and X-ray Institute started in 1911. Mr. E.S. Hoare, a British diagnostic x-ray technician, came to Calgary and Dr. McGuffin's clinic, circa 1911. In Dr. W.B. Parsons' article on Dr. William Herbert McGuffin, in A New Kind of Ray, pages 157-162, 260, he outlines how significant a contributor Dr. McGuffin was to Radiology and cancer care in North America. Dr. Parsons suggested Dr. McGuffin began his radiology career in 1912 and served as a radiologist during WWI, before specializing in radiology in 1918.

29 Letts, H. — The Edmonton Academy of Medicine: a History, page 5.

30 Parsons, W.B. — Information on The Early Days of Radiology in Alberta, pages 4-5.

31 Stanley, G.D. — Dr. George Malcolmson, pages 82-83.

32 Stanley, G.D. — Dr. George Malcolmson, page 81.

33 Stanley, G.D. — Dr. George Malcolmson, page 80.

34 Jamieson, H.C. — Early Medicine in Alberta, page 131.

35 Chatenay, H. — Dr. George Henry Malcolmson, in The Country Doctors, page 17, Matrix Press, 1980.

36 Jamieson, H.C. — Early Medicine in Alberta, page 131.

General References:

Arnold, Hugh A. — Frank Hamilton Mewburn. Paper read to the Whoop-Up Chapter of the Historical Society of Alberta April 29, 1975. Reprinted in the Lethbridge Historical Society Newsletter, 1991, #6.

Beahen, William & Horrall, Stan — Red Coats on the Prairies, Centax Books, 1998.

Bergin, Darby — The Medical and Surgical History of the Canadian North-West Rebellion of 1885. John Lovell, 1886.

Bishop, W.J. — The early History of Surgery, Robert Hale, 1960.

Campbell, Peter M. — Frank Hamilton Mewburn, CACHB 15(4): 63-68, 1951.

Campbell, Peter M. — The Honourable L.G. deVeber. Alberta Medical Bulletin 14(3): 43-44, 1949.

Chatenay, Henry — Dr. George Malcolmson, in the Country Doctors, Matrix Press, 1980.

Dempsey, Hugh A. — The letters of Dr. R.B. Nevitt, in A Winter at Fort Macleod, Glenbow, 1974.

Higinbotham, John D. — When the West Was Young, Ryerson 1933. Reprinted by Bruce Haig, 1978.

Jamieson, Heber C. — Early Medicine in Alberta, AMA, 1947.

Johnston, Alex, et al — Lethbridge Its Medical Doctors, Dentists, Drug Stores, Occasional Paper #24 Lethbridge Historical Society, 1991.

Kerr, Robert B. — The History of the Medical Council of Canada, MCC, 1979.

Kerr William J. — Frank Slide, 1990.

Kittson, John G. — Report of Surgeon John Kittson, Swan River, December 19, 1875. Reprinted in A Chronicle of the Canadian West, Historical Society of Alberta, 1975.

Lampard, Robert — First and second Canadian Medical Association meetings in Alberta/NWT, August 11-12, 1889 and August 10-14, 1912. Alberta Doctors Digest 29: 4-9, July/August 2004 and 30(1): 4-8, January/February 2005.

Lampard, Robert — Profiles and Perspectives from Alberta's Medical History. Two volumes to be published in 2006.

McDougall, Gerald M. — Physicians and Medical Clinics in Southern Alberta, University of Calgary, 1991.

Mewburn, Frank H. — The Life and Work of Dr. George A. Kennedy, CMAJ 21: 327-330, 1929.

Neatby, Hilda — The Medical Profession in the North West Territories, Saskatchewan History 2(2): 1-15, May 1949.

NWMP Annual Reports — Surgeon Reports appended to the Annual Reports 1874-1889. Reprinted in four volumes, Coles Canadiana, 1973.

Rawlinson, H.E. — Frank Hamilton Mewburn, Canadian Journal of Surgery 2: 1-5, October 1958.

Scarlett, Earle P., & Stanley George D. Editors — Calgary Associate Clinic Historical Bulletin (CACHB), Volumes 21-24. 1956-1958 (NWMP).

Stanley, George D. — Dr. George Malcolmson, CACHB 14(4): 78-85, February 1950.

Tolten, Gordon E. — The Rocky Mountain Rangers, Occasional Paper #28, Lethbridge Historical Society, 1994.

Index

The Author:

Dr. Robert Lampard, MD

Dr. Robert Lampard's interest in Alberta's history began as an Historical Society of Alberta (HSA) member in 1968. A native of Red Deer, he has chaired the Red Deer Museum and Fort Normandeau Boards, the Historical Preservation Committee and the Central Alberta Historical Society as well as being a board member since the HSA Chapter inception in 1994. Projects in which he has been involved include: the saving of the CPR Bridge, the W.O. Mitchell Black Bonspiel mural in the Red Deer Curling Club and the Historic Arches Park in downtown Red Deer.

Alberta's history and most significantly the history of medicine has benefited greatly through the efforts of historian Dr. Lampard. He received his medical degree from the University of Alberta in 1964, Master Science (Surgery) degree at the University of Alberta in 1967 and his Master of Business Administration (MBA) from the University of Western Ontario in 1968. He served as the medical director of the Foothills Hospital in Calgary from 1968 to 1981 and the Michener Centre in Red Deer since 1983. Since 1995, Dr. Lampard has been president of the Alberta Medical Foundation (AMF), which funds and documents Alberta's medical history. Dr. Lampard, Dr. Hugh Arnold of Lethbridge and Dr. Don Wilson of Edmonton with a few others, were instrumental in founding the Alberta Medical Foundation (AMF) in 1987.

As a medical historian he has contributed articles on early physicians to Alberta History on Drs. James Hector, Robert Brett and Calgary Rotarian James Wheeler Davidson. He contributed articles to the Alberta Doctors Digest on the first four Canadian Medical Association conventions in Alberta in 1889,

1912, 1934, 1942. He has been a member of the Archives Committee of the AMA and its successor the Alberta Medical Foundation (AMF) almost continually since 1981. At the University of Calgary (UofC) he has been a preceptor in the medical history course for over a decade, and chaired the committee that established the Alberta medical history website at the UofC www.ourfutureourpast.ca. He has participated in selection of the Canadian Medical Historian of the Year, been a recipient of the Dr. W.B. Spaulding Certificate of Merit for contributions to Canadian Medical History and granted a life membership in the Canadian Medical Association.

As part of Alberta's centennial celebrations in 2005, the Alberta Medical Association (AMA) and College of Physicians and Surgeons appointed a panel of fourteen judges to select 100 Alberta Physicians of the Century. Dr. Lampard nominated many of the physicians that were recognized. Dr. Lampard himself, was surprised and honoured to be selected as one of the 100 Alberta Physicians of the Century.

Dr. Lampard currently has four books in progress on: The Life and Times of James and Lillian Davidson in Rotary International; Profiles and Perspectives from Alberta's Medical History (2 vol.); and this volume on early physicians in Southern Alberta. Residing in Red Deer, Dr. Lampard is married to Sharon. They have three children. Son Bruce is a physician with MSF (Doctors Without Borders). Geoffrey is presently at McGill University in the Science program. Daughter Allison is a grade 12 student continuing her studies through the Rotary International Youth Exchange Program.